eForth and Zen

Dr. C. H. Ting

Third Edition

Offete Enterprises
2016

It is part of the current Forth Bookshelf and can be found at
https://www.amazon.co.uk/Juergen-Pintaske/e/B00N8HVEZM

1 **Charles Moore** - Forth - The Early Years: Background information about the beginnings of this Computer Language
2 **Charles Moore** - Programming A Problem Oriented Language: Forth - how the internals work
3 **Leo Brodie** - Starting Forth -The Classic
4 **Leo Wong** – **Juergen Pintaske** – **Stephen Pelc** FORTH LITE TUTORIAL: Code tested with free MPE VFX Forth, SwiftForth and Gforth
5 **Juergen Pintaske** – **A START WITH FORTH** - Bits to Bites Collection – 12 Words to start, then 35 Words, Javascript Forth on the Web, more
6 **Stephen Pelc** - Programming Forth: Version July 2016
7 **Brad Rodriguez** - Moving Forth / TTL CPU / B.Y.O. Assembler
8 **Tim Hentlass** - Real Time Forth

9 **Chen-Hanson Ting** - Footsteps In An Empty Valley issue 3
10 **Chen-Hanson Ting** - Zen and the Forth Language: EFORTH for the MSP430G2552 from Texas Instruments
11 **Chen-Hanson Ting** - eForth and Zen - 3rd Edition 2017: with 32-bit 86eForth v5.2 for Visual Studio 2015
12 **Chen-Hanson Ting** - eForth Overview
13 **Chen-Hanson Ting** - FIG-Forth Manual Document /Test in 1802 IP
14 **Chen-Hanson Ting** - EP32 RISC Processor IP: Description and Implementation into FPGA – ASIC tested by NASA
15 **Chen-Hanson Ting** – Irriducible Complexity
16 **Chen-Hanson Ting** - Arduino controlled by eForth
17 **Chen-Hanson Ting** – eForth as Arduino Sketch – no Programmer needed

18 **Burkhard Kainka** - Learning Programming with MyCo: Learning Programming easily - independent of a PC (Forth code to follow soon)
19 **Burkhard Kainka** - BBC Micro:bit: Tests Tricks Secrets Code, Additional MicroBit information when running the Mecrisp Package
20 **Burkhard Kainka** – **Thomas Baum** – Web Programming ATYTINY13
21 **Georg Heinrichs** - The ATTINY Project – Why Forth?
22 **Dr. Karl Meinzer** - IPS, a Forth-like language for Space

Juergen Pintaske, publisher, June 2020

Contents

Chapter 4. Assemble eForth on Visual Studio   **58**

Chapter 5. eForth Virtual Forth Engine   **74**

Chapter 6. eForth Kernel   **95**

https://wiki.forth-ev.de/doku.php/projects:ep32:start for more info

File: 86eforth502_J_v11_2017_02_19.doc 2020
Email feedback to epldfpga@aol.com

Preface to the Third Edition

86eForth v1.0 was released in 1990 for a 16-bit 8086 microprocessor, and in 1993 I wrote the first edition of this book to serve as the manual of eForth Model. In 1996, after Intel released 80386, I felt the urge to modify it for a 32-bit 386 CPU. After much struggle with the real and protected modes, I realized that PC with 386 CPU was a mainframe computer destined for Windows, and would never be an embedded system for applications I was interested in. I abandoned PC and turned to other more interesting microcontrollers and Forth processors.

Around 2000, Cheah-shen Yap in Taiwan FIG expanded the 32-bit 86eForth v4.3 to F# with full Windows interface. It was a very pleasant system for Windows environment, and I used it for all my programming applications on Windows. Unfortunately, Microsoft hijacked the name F#, and we had no means to fight back.

Recently, I closed down www.offete.com, and much of the eForth system it distributed were unavailable to Forth users. Many friends asked about this and that. Many were inquiring about this book. Juergen Pinstake edited a portion of it and posted on Amazon as *eForth Overview*. After re-writing eForth for many microcontrollers, and trying to optimize it for various applications, I always felt that eForth and Zen was outdated, but never found the time and energy to revise it.

In 2016, I had an opportunity to review the evolution of 86eForth, and found that I could still assemble 86eForth v1.0 and ran it on my old Windows XP machine, but the assembled code would not run on my Windows 7 laptop. I thought that if I were to revise *eForth and Zen*, I should have a version of 86eForth which would run on current Windows PC, and use it as the basis of *eForth and Zen*.

In late 2015, Amazon had a Christmas special of Fire tablets for only $35. I bought a bunch for my grandkids, and saved one for myself. Fire is a marvelous tablet with nice color display, sound and camera. I would love to run Forth on it. I heard that Microsoft just released

Visual Studio 2015 Community, which was a multiple language IDE capable of developing Android application for Fire. I downloaded Visual Studio, and found there were so much to learn to build Windows applications, and I was so much outdated.

There was at least one thing I could do and that's updating 86eForth. I found that Microsoft was no longer supporting MASM, but buried it as ml.exe under C++ in Visual Studio 2015. With the help of Kip Irvine's book *Assembly Language for x86 Processors*, and the code library he distributed, I could still write assembly code for 386 and test it. However, the 32-bit 86eForth v4.3 did not work, because ML imposes much stricter rules on memory segmentation. It requires you to declare 3 segments:

```
.stack
.code
.data
```

You have to put your program in .code segment, and all your variables in .data segment. You can put constants in .code segment if you will not change them at run time. You cannot add new code in .code segment, and you cannot execute code in .data segment.

Forth is an extensible language, and you have to add new words to extend it. That's how you program in Forth. Restricting the usage of .code and .data segments denies you the privilege to run Forth in such environment. While converting 86eForth v4.3 to ML assembly, I looked for ways to circumvent this code/data segment restriction, but to no success. In the end, I decided to change 86eForth from direct thread model to indirect thread model. In the original 86eForth v1.0, it used direct thread model, which had no parameter field, and code field contains executable code and necessary data. Parameter field was not necessary, and the system was simpler, more concise and faster. On the other hand, in indirect thread model, code field and parameter field in colon words contains no executable code. They have only address pointers. Therefore, I can add new colon words to .data segment at will. The address interpreter can process the token list in the parameter field of colon words. As far as ML assembler is concerned, colon words are pure data, and it does not mind whether I put them in .code segment or .data segment.

In 86eForth v5.1, I successfully ported 86eForth v4.3 to ML, with direct thread model. In 86eForth v5.2, indirect thread model was adopted. Earlier in 1996, I tried to simplify 86eForth v1.0 by deleting multitasking and CATCH-THROW error handling features, which were rarely used in embedded applications. These changes were also incorporated in 86eForth v5.2. Word count was reduced from 223 to 181, and I thought that I had reached the stage of Irreducible Complexity.

I had another concern about *eForth and Zen*, which was that I used Forth pseudo-code in explaining the functions of high level colon words. In writing 86eForth v1.0, Bill Muench gave me his bForth source code in Forth. He was metacompiling his bForth. That was, he ran a version of bForth on PC, and from it he compiled a new bForth written in Forth. I paraphrased his bForth to MASM assembly. At that time, I felt very comfortable in using his Forth pseudo-code to describe eForth. Later, my feeling changed, and thought it was unfair to require your having some elementary knowledge of Forth before reading *eForth and Zen*. Now is the right time to make the leap. In this new edition, I will follow the assembly code faithfully, and assume that you have no prior knowledge of Forth. If you only knew 80386 assembly, you could follow the discussion without any problem.

The last problem I had with *eForth and Zen* was the format in presenting assembly source code, comments and more detailed explanation. I wrote many eForth manuals for different microcontrollers. Every time I tried changing the format slightly to better facilitate the discussion. I would like to fill the pages with useful information, leaving the least amount of empty space. In this edition, I think I got the best format under Microsoft Word. Here is an example, in which I have invisible borders around various fields:

DUMP dumps 128 bytes starting at address b to the terminal. It dumps 16 bytes to a line. A line begins with the address of the first byte, followed by 16 bytes shown in hex, 3 columns per bytes. At the end of a line are the 16 bytes shown in ASCII code. Non-printable characters by replaced by underscores.

	ON	UMP' , DUMP	P (a --) Dump 128 bytes from a, ormatted manner.
		T , 7	ɡe count to lines
			count down loop
1:		UPP , DOLIT , 8 , UDOTR	ʌy address
		E , DOLIT , 15	ı space
2:		T , DOLIT , 3 , UDOTR	ʌy 16 bytes of data
		T , DUMP2	
		E , DUPP	pace
		T , 16 , SUBBB	
		T , 16 , TYPES	ʌy 16 byte of text
		T , DUMP1	till done
		'	
		T	

In the top horizontal field, I describe the intended function of a word. I can add text and graphics freely in this field. Under the top horizontal field, 4 vertical fields are used to show assembly label, assembly code, assembly arguments, and comments, from left to right. These 4 lower fields are basically what you see in assembly code. The first cell in an argument field is the header of a word, preceded by macro command $CODE or $COLON in the code field. I moved two whole line comments in assembly source with stack pictures before a word to the right of the corresponding header. In the label, code and argument fields, I set font to Courier New to show that these characters are source code to be assembled. In the comment field, I set font to Times New Roman, to show that they are ignored by ML assembler. I also deleted the ';' character required by ML to start comments.

I am very happy with the format, and I hope you like it as much as I do.

Happy Forthing!
Chen-Hanson Ting - San Mateo, California, September 2016

Chapter 1. - Forth and Zen

Forth is often mentioned not only as a computer language but also a religion, because of its feverish followers. Among the religions, Zen is considered to be the closest to Forth. As popularly known, Zen is understood as a synonym of simplicity, brevity, light, understanding, wisdom and enlightenment. These are also attributes to Forth as a language and a philosophy. Indeed, Zen and Forth also bear striking similarity in their historical development and evolution. This aspect of similarity between Forth and Zen has not been well documented, and this is one purpose of this paper.

Zen and Forth both started as revolutions towards well entrenched establishments--the priesthood. Zen and Forth both started as oral traditions because of the lack in supporting literature and the high concentration of expertise.

Zen and Forth both stressed that their matters of subject were simple and straightforward. However, it was in the interests of the entrenched establishment to make things complicated and inaccessible to common folks.

Zen and Forth both stressed that the true enlightenment and understanding were within the grasp of individuals. The rituals and the accepted practices exercised in the establishments had nothing to do with these goals.

Here I would like to compare Zen and Forth in greater details so that we all have a better appreciation of these two seemingly unrelated topics. Forth programmers may be encouraged to press on using this language with a higher hope that their work will be recognized by their peers in the future.

Comparing Forth and Zen

The most important contributions of Huineng, the Sixth Patriarch of Zen in China, was that he had his lectures recorded by his disciples. He also had the lectures printed and distributed as identifications of discipleship to his teach and his philosophy. In striking contrast to the Buddhist Sutras translated from Sanskrit, the lectures were plain, easy to read and to comprehend. This collection of lectures was the only book written by a Chinese to be granted the status of a Sutra in the Buddhist literature, and is commonly call the Platform Sutra. (Sutras were the teaching of Buddha himself.)

People compared Forth and Zen in a very superficial manner, mostly without the understanding of either. I feel that there is a need to treat both subjects fully in a single treatise. There is no better way than to present the very original text of Zen and the source code of Forth side by side. In the course of preparing the complete documentation for eForth, I thought it would be very useful to lay down the eForth text in parallel with the original text of the Platform Sutra. Of course, it is impossible to correlate the text of eForth directly with the text of the Platform Sutra. However, one should be able to see the common threads in them, as the themes of simplicity, personal understanding, enlightenment, and the struggles against prevailing established doctrines recurring time and again in both texts.

As I intended this book for both English and Chinese readers, I would like to include texts and discussions in both English and Chinese. In effect, we would have four threads running in parallel: the original Platform Sutra in Chinese, its English translation, the text of eForth, and its Chinese translation. This is how this book is laid out.

Historically, Zen was a grand synthesis, combining the essence of Buddhism, Confucianism, and Taoism after about one thousand years of inter fertilization. It was the results of the many Chinese minds, struggling for emancipation after a thousand years of conflicts between the traditional humanistic Confucianism, the nihilistic Taoism and the imported anti-materialistic Buddhism. It laid dormant for a hundred years, surviving through five generations of Zen masters, passing the doctrine orally from heart to heart.

Eventually, during the reign of the Sixth Patriarch, Huineng (638-714 AD), it blossomed in full and became the dominating religious philosophy in China ever since. Its influence spread into Japan, Korea, and Southeast Asia. Lately, it also became fashionable in Western Europe and America.

The history of Forth is too short for meaningful comparison with that of Zen. It was virtually unknown to the world in its first decade of existence until the late 70's. It was invented by a lone programmer, Charles H. Moore, outside of the main stream of computer industry and computer sciences. In the early 70's, it was only used in astronomy, as he helped programming minicomputers to automate telescopes and observatories. Then it blossomed with microcomputer revolution, promoted by Forth Interest Group in the early 1980's. Since 1985, the Forth Interest Group has been in steady decline, as C became the dominant programming language. The advantages of Forth, such as elegance in its architecture, simplicity in its syntactic construction, and economy in memory utilization, seem irrelevant in the age of mega-resources, where MIPS, megabytes of RAM memory, gigabytes of disk storage are commodities easily affordable.

As the operating systems and applications grow to fill the available RAM and disk storage, at some point people will ask the question whether these huge programs are worthy of the resources they consume. People will have to ask whether the direction we are heading will lead us to better lives and better environment. When we stop equating bigger to better, and more to happier, then we can re-evaluate the computer technology in a new light. Then, maybe Forth will shine again.

Zen as an Oral Tradition

Buddhism was founded by Gautama Siddhartha, a religious philosopher and teacher who lived in India (~560-480 B.C.) He was called Buddha which means the enlightened one. He attracted a large following. His teaching in essence was that one could reach Nirvana, a divine state of release from earthly pain, sorrow, and desire, by the right living, the right thinking and self denial. He left no writing behind, while Buddhism flourished in India for a long time.

The meaning of Zen is meditation. Why meditate? To achieve enlightenment. What is enlightenment? Nobody really knows, and nobody can tell. The best story about Zen and enlightenment was that one day Śākyamuni Buddha (~500BC), the original enlightened one, lifted a flower to show his disciples. Nobody knew what he meant. Only Mahākāśyapa smiled and Buddha announced that Mahākāśyapa got enlightened. So the story was told that the enlightenment passed on from Mahākāśyapa through 28 generations of masters, until Budhidharma brought it to China.

In the two hundred years after Buddha's death, many schools formed after different personalities and there were great arguments and debates concerning what were his true teaching. Great conventions were held to debate the issues and codified his teachings as Sutras in Sanskrit.

The earlier dominant school was Hinayana, which spread to the south and is still flourishing in Sri Lanka, Burma, and Thailand. The later dominant school was Mahayana, which spread into China, Tibet, Korea, and Japan.

The Hinayana School emphasize the mystic power of Buddha and the personal salvation through one's own efforts. The Mahayana School emphasized eclecticism and in common search for salvation.

After the introduction of Mahayana into China in 200 AD, it arose great interests in the intellectuals as well as the peasants. Many emperors and their courts were converted and spent great efforts in building temples and spreading the Buddhism. A continuing effort over three hundred years was devoted to translate Sanskrit Sutra and related literature into Chinese. In Tang Dynasty (618-907 AD), more than 5000 volumes of Buddhist literature were translated and assembled.

Most of the Sutra translations were done poorly and required a priesthood for the interpretation and dissimulation. The vast amount of literature also caused sectarian divisions and arguments among the priesthood, continuing the Hindu tradition.

Zen was introduced into China by a legendary Indian monk Buddhidharma in 527 AD. He stayed at the Shaolin Temple for 9 years, spending all his time meditating in front of a stone wall. He was known as the 'Indian Monk Looking at a Wall'. He didn't use any Sutra, and he didn't write anything. He taught a few students and encouraged them to find enlightenment in themselves. His teaching was summarized as:

教外别传,	*My teaching is outside Buddhist tradition,*
不立文字,	*As truth cannot be conveyed by writings;*
直指人心,	*Cleanse your mind to reveal your true nature;*
见性成佛.	*You can reach Nirvana directly.*

Buddhidharma passed his garment and bowl to his student Huiko as evidence of the discipleship and commanded him to do the same for five generations. He then returned to India. Huiko passed the teach with the garment and the bowl to Sengtsan. Sengtsan passed them to Taohsin. Taohsin passed them to Hungjen. Finally, Hungjen passed them to Huineng (638-714 AD).

For a hundred years, Zen was passed from mouth to mouth, and from heart to heart. Very few people knew of its existence. Even fewer knew its philosophy and teachings. In China, Buddhism flourished when supported by the emperors and by high officers. A number of times the Buddhism was almost completely destroyed when the country was in turmoil and when the Confucian officers could convince the emperor that Buddhists were threats to the state. All the while, the Zen masters orally passed their teachings from one generation to the next.

Forth as an Oral Tradition

Forth was invented by Charles (Chuck) H. Moore who was trained as a physicist in MIT but wandered into programming. In early days, he built an interpreter so that it would execute words on punched cards. Later he found that these words could be more conveniently compiled into lists, which could be executed by the computer more conveniently. The interpreter with very little modifications, could be made to compile anything and everything, and the whole scheme evolved into a programming language. It was named Forth, as abbreviated from Fourth, meaning the fourth generation of programming language when the third generation of computers bases on integrated circuits were becoming prevailing in the computing industry.

Very early in the development of Forth, a state of closure was reached. Chuck was able to generate new Forth systems from an existing Forth system through meta-compilation. He did not need other programming tools to build new Forth systems, and Forth started to evolve independent of the existing operating systems and programming languages. This state of closure was very interesting, like the ying-yang cycle. One could not find an entry point once the cycle was closed. In that Chuck had the monopoly on Forth, because very few people possessed the understanding to cut in the cycle in order to build new Forth systems. He felt quite secure in giving users the complete source listings, fairly sure of that nobody could reversed engineered the Forth technology, even though the source listings were complete and truthful.

Indeed, the source code was very difficult to read, because a Forth system was generated by the meta-compiler, and the meta-compiler was written in Forth. To understand Forth, one had to understand the meta-compiler. To understand the meta-compiler, one had to understand Forth completely. Where do you start?

Forth thus became a legend. The astronomers loved it so much that they made it the standard language for observatory automation. It was fairly easy to use but very difficult to understand. The source code traveled to the far corners of the world with the telescopes, but the knowledge and understanding of Forth was only passed from mouth to mouth and heart to heart. Hence Forth became an oral tradition these days. Forth code tended to be concise and often packed tightly in blocks. In-line documentation and comments were deemed too expensive, and most code was poorly commented. Forth thus acquired the reputation of a write-only language.

Several manuals were circulated among the observatories, documenting a few of the most popular Forth implementations. These manuals mostly contained a short section introducing Forth and discussing how to use that particular Forth system, and a long dictionary documenting what each word did. These manuals told the users what Forth was, but provided very little help as to how Forth worked.

Acceptance of Zen

Huineng, the Sixth Patriarch, was a genius. He couldn't read because he was borne poor and gathered wood for a living, but he could explain the Sutras when people read them to him. He went to learn from the Fifth Patriarch Hungjen, and Hungjen sent him to labor in the kitchen. As Hungjen got old and wanted to pass on his garment and bowl, he asked his students to write poems to show him their understanding of enlightenment. His best student Shenhsiu wrote the following poem:

身是菩提树，   *My body is the bodhi tree,*
心为明镜台。   *And my mind a mirror bright.*
时时勤拂拭，   *Carefully I wipe them hour by hour,*
勿使惹尘埃"。   *And let no dust alight.*

Hearing this poem, Huineng asked a scholar to write down his own poem, because he couldn't write himself:

菩提本无树，	*There is no bodhi tree,*
明镜亦非台，	*Nor stand of a mirror bright.*
本来无一物，	*Since all is void,*
何处惹尘埃。	*Where can the dust alight?*

When Hungjen saw this poem, he passed his garment and bowl to Huineng and told Huineng: "You are the one Buddhidharma prophesied. Zen will flourish in China through you. Take the garment and bowl to be the Sixth Patriarch, but do not pass them on any more." Hungjen was in such a hurry to pass things to Huineng that he didn't even shave Huineng's hair (to admit him to Buddhist order), as Huineng was still a layman.

About 20 years later, when Huineng was well established as the Master of Zen, he was asked by a Provincial Officer to give lectures on Zen. The Officer had Huineng's eldest student Fahai recorded his lectures and had the lectures distributed as the *Platform Sutra, Lectures by the Six Patriarch*. When Huineng was about to die, Fahai asked him: "What are you going to do with your garment and bowl? Who's going the inherit them?" Huineng said: "As commanded by Buddhidharma, the garment and bowl will not be passed on. But now you have the *Platform Sutra*. Go forth and teach others according to this Sutra. Everything I learned I put down in it. When you read it, it is as if you are listening to me."

20 years after Huineng died, the Northern School of Zen was favored by the royal court and dominated the Buddhist landscape. The Southern School of Zen was scattered and mute in Southern China. One of Huineng's student, Shenhui (686-760 AD), went to the capital and challenged the doctrine and the Zen inheritance of the Northern School in a series of lectures and public debates. He convinced the court and the public of the historical significance of Huineng and established the *Platform Sutra* as the orthodox doctrine of Zen Buddhism.

Acceptance of Forth

The major breakthrough in the Forth arena was due to the Forth Interest Group, which was founded by Bill Ragsdale in 1978 in the Silicon Valley. The most important contribution FIG made was to reverse-engineer a Forth system from ground zero, thus breaking the infinite ying-yang cycle. FIG organized a Forth Implementation Team which built and released 6 Forth implementations for the 6 then most popular microprocessors based on the figForth model. These implementations were written in assembly code of the native microprocessors. People who were familiar with assembly code could then easily implement figForth on their own microcomputers. figForth thus trained a new generation of Forth programmers outside the Forth oral tradition.

There was a host of Forth literature appearing in the early 1980's, which further helped the popularization of Forth among the personal computer users. Among them was Leo Brodie's *Starting Forth* , *Thinking Forth*, and the *1979 Special Forth Language Issue* in the Byte magazine. *Forth Dimensions* from FIG and *Journal of Forth Applications and Research* from the Forth Institute were the two major publications on Forth. These literature showed that Forth penetrated into many different scientific communities and technical industries.

My most important contribution to Forth was the publication of *Systems Guide to figForth*, first released in 1979. Instead of telling people what Forth did, it systematically explored how Forth did things and why things were done the ways they were. It put to rest the myth that Forth was a *write-only language* by showing that Forth could be understood by averaged user with somewhat casual studying. It showed how the inner interpreter and the outer interpreter worked, and why words and dictionary in Forth were constructed the ways they were by necessity. It proved that the understanding of Forth could be transmitted through paper medium without personal interaction. The impact of this work, I would like to believe myself, was similar to what Huineng caused with his *Platform Sutra* on Zen.

Simplicity in Zen

Buddhism is very complicated because it is not a monolithic system of thoughts and philosophy. It accumulated many centuries of cultural and philosophical development. The Sutras were all attributed to Buddha but were most likely written by people remotely associated with him. Lots of mystic Hinduism found their ways into Buddhism, which was inevitable because Buddhism was developed in the Hindu environment, like the 33 layers of heaven, 18 layers of hell, the reincarnation of all animals, etc.

There were many different theories about life, death, and Nirvana. There were many sectors and schools about how one could attain Nirvana to avoid the reincarnation into a lower animal form. Thing got complicated and confusion reigned supreme. In essence, everybody just picked what he believed and convinced others that his was the best and most logical way to deal with life and all its ramifications.

The general consensus was that vegetarianism was good, giving to the temple was good, kindness to people and animal was good, reciting Sutra was good, meditation was good, worshipping Buddha and other Buddhist deities was good, dedicating to priesthood was good, etc. Could one attain Nirvana by doing all these? Maybe. Maybe not.

Zen was a great simplification of all these. Huineng maintained that Buddha hood and enlightenment could not be achieved through generally accepted Buddhist practices, like reciting Sutras, making offerings, meditation in special sitting positions. As everybody already had the Buddha nature in him, all he had to do is looking inward to find the true Buddha. Our senses and our thoughts tended to veil us from the Buddha nature and they should not be trusted. The process of Zen (Dhyana, Ch'an, meditation), was to reject the influences of senses and thoughts, and to arrive at a state of ideallessness, nonobjectivity, and nonattachment. In this state, nothing external of ourselves and within our own minds can influence us and dragged us back to the earthy existence.

Simplicity in Forth

The poem by Shenhsiu and the poem by Huineng provide the best contrast for us to compare the conventional wisdom in the current computer industry against the Forth philosophy. Digital computers evolved for more than 70 years and there are hundreds of different architectures and designs. And, there are hundreds of operating systems and programming languages. Manuals, documentation, books, tools, and applications fill library shelves and computer book stores. All universities open departments of computer sciences and related subject. One can be easily overwhelmed with information.

Computer hardware is difficult. Computer software is even more difficult. We have volumes and volumes of literature to prove them. Hardware and software are difficult, only because people are not given the right tools to deal with the complexity in these systems. If we insist on asking whether the complexity is necessary, we can convince ourselves that they should not be complicated. The computer hardware evolved trying to solve the perceived software problems. The software evolved trying to solve the perceived hardware problems and the problems in the human interface. If these preconceived problems do not exist at all, the hardware can be simple and powerful. The software can be simple and powerful as well.

In a typical computer system, there are layers upon layers of software between you and the computer hardware. The operating system and its utilities, the compilers, assemblers, editors, linkers and loaders are all very complicated and mostly proprietary programs. They helped you starting your journey into this computer juggle. After a while, they tend to hinder your progress, because they insulate you from the hardware, and deliberate efforts were expended to prevent you to fully make use of the capabilities built in the hardware.

This issue of simplicity can be illustrated in the following diagram. The operating systems and the applications separate you from the computer hardware. The software protects the hardware, because the user is not to be trusted. Leaving to the user, he will abuse the hardware and causes the system to crash. In the days of mainframe computers, the greatest sin was to crash the computer, because the livelihood of the computer priesthood depended upon the continuing operation of the computer. The hardware and the operating system had to be protected at all costs.

In this age of personal computers, the priority is turned by 180 degrees. You own the computer. You are responsible for its operation. Is it necessary to protect the computer against you?

Forth provides a much simplified interface between you and your computer as show in the following diagram. Forth is a simple and integrated interface between you and your computer. Through Forth, you can directly control the computer hardware, because every part of the computer system is freely accessible to you. Therefore, you can explore the best way to use the computer system to suit your applications.

With the freedom to access computer hardware comes the responsibility to use the hardware properly. You may crash the system frequently. It will cause no harm as long as the computer can recover quickly from the crashes with minimal damages to the data stored in the computer system. After all, you own the computer.

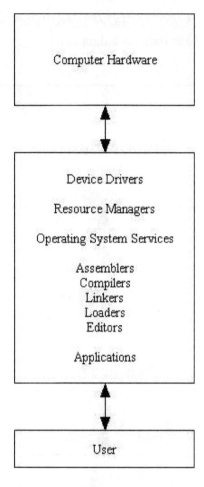

There are other examples which show that complexity does not necessarily mean performance. Simple systems are generally faster and more resilient.

Registers in the CPU are designed to hold temporary data so that the CPU does not have to go to the slow memory to fetch and store data. However, too many registers become a burden when you call subroutines, and the registers must be saved before calling and restored after returning. In order to speed up a computer, you tend to have more and more registers and make less and less subroutine calls. If we recognize that in high level languages and in structure programming, the subroutine is the most important mechanism, we should instead optimize the memory access in subroutine call-return and put all intermediate data on a data stack.

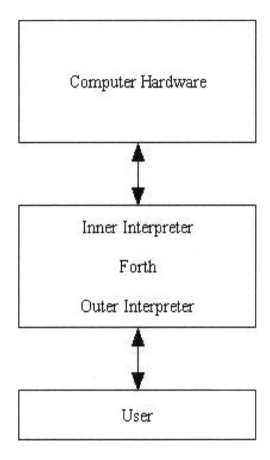

Another example is the prefix arithmetical notation prevailing in conventional programming languages. The prefix notation is unnatural and was forced upon all young minds in their algebra lessons. It is much more natural for both computers and humans to think in linear lists, sequentially executed. Thinking algebraically, you need a two-pass compiler to break the equations down into pieces and reassemble them for the computer to execute. Thinking in the postfix terms, a simple one-pass interpreter can be created to perform all the functions required of a complicated compiler.

Enlightenment in Zen

Zen was the cumulative synthesis of the Buddhist philosophy with traditional Chinese Confucianism and Taoism. Zen was also a revolution against the Buddhist traditions and establishments. It discredited the Buddhist practices, which emphasized ceremonies and outer appearances, while claimed that the enlightenment exists only in the minds of individuals.

A huge amount of Buddhist literature had been translated from Sanskrit to Chinese. Because the translations were difficult to understand, a priesthood was established for its dissimulation and interpretation. Towards this literal tradition, the Zen masters proclaimed that enlightenment could not be transmitted by written words, but had to be handed done orally from heart to heart.

In traditional Buddhist theories, it was very difficult to attain Nirvana or Buddha-hood. It required a long time of studying, meditation, and the practice of self-denial. In the end, there was still no assurance that one could attain it. Even if one attained it in this life, there would be the possibility of losing it in the next life. There were external forces which we could not know and we could not avoid.

Zen placed the possibility and the capability to attain enlightenment and Buddha-hood squarely on the individual, by declaring that the Buddha nature is part of the human nature and it exists in everybody. The Buddha nature is vile and corrupted by the worldly desires and thoughts. These desires and thoughts can be purged, the individual can thus be enlightened, and his own Buddha nature can reveal itself. The enlightenment is the realization of this self-sufficient Buddha nature.

As to how one became enlightened, there were two major schools of thoughts. Huineng insisted that enlightenment came suddenly and Senghsui maintained that it ought to be the results of diligent study, mediation and searching. These were the Southern Sudden School and the Northern Gradual School. However, as Huineng maintained, how enlightenment is achieved is not important. The important thing is its realization. People are all different, and they are enlightened in different ways. A master can teach, but he cannot enlighten. The enlightenment comes from within. The best a master can do is to inspire, to help, to lead the way, and maybe to strike a sharp blow on the head at the right time.

Enlightenment in Forth

What is the enlightenment in Forth? I think it is the complete understanding of a computer in terms of its operations and its interface to you. This understanding is not as complicated as we have all being led to believe. It involves two components of Forth: the inner interpreter which Forth imposes on computer hardware to execute Forth lists, and the outer interpreter which executes words you typed in. If you understand both the inner interpreter and the outer interpreter, you have the complete understanding of computers, in the sense that you can go out and build a Forth system on any computer and make that computer do what you want it to do. You then will realize that operating systems and languages enslave you to do what the system permits you to do, while Forth gives you freedom to tell the computer to do what you want to do. This is enlightenment.

Operating systems and programming languages are designed to enslave you, by their sheer sizes and their complexities. They are too complicated to be understood by individual users. Forth shows that an operating system and a high level language do not have to be complicated. In fact, they can be very simple and can be mastered by individuals with some limited efforts. Once the principles are mastered, they can be applied to all computers. Then, you become the master, and the computers become obedient but powerful slaves. To be the master of powerful slaves is very enlightening and satisfying. Once you taste the freedom and the satisfaction of being the master, you will not want to be enslaved again by a computer through its operating systems and programming languages.

Chapter 2. - What is Forth?

Forth was invented by Chuck Moore in the 1960s as a programming language. Chuck was not impressed by programming languages, operating systems, and computer hardware of his time. He sought the simplest and most efficient way to control his computers. He used Forth to program every computer in his sight. And then, he found that he could design better computers, because Forth is much more than just a programming language; it is an excellent computer architecture.

Although Forth is a programming language to program computers, it is very similar to natural languages like English. Forth has a set of commands, similar to words in English. Forth commands therefore are called words. Hereafter, I will use commands or words interchangeably. Forth has a very simple grammar rule: words are separated by blanks. A Forth computer processes lists of words, executing words from left to right. It is like English: you read a sentence from left to right.

Forth is like a natural language, in which new words are defined in terms of existing words. Adding new words extends the language, pushes it towards higher and higher levels of abstraction, eventually solving all computable problems. It is the simplest and most powerful form of intelligence, essentially the way how human beings think, reason, communicate, and accumulate knowledge.

Among programming languages, Forth is very close to LISP. Both assume that computable problems can be best solved in nested lists. LISP solves a problem from top down, and it uses lots of parentheses to enclose nested lists. Forth solves a problem from bottom up. It replaces lists of existing words/lists with new words.

A more detailed and precise description of Forth is as follows:

- Forth has a set of words or commands.

- Forth words are records stored in a computer memory area, called a dictionary.

- A Forth word has two representations: an external representation in the form of an ASCII name; and an internal representation in the form of a token, which invokes executable code stored in memory.

- There are two principal types of Forth words: low level code words containing machine instructions, and high level colon words containing token lists.

- Forth has a text interpreter, which scans a list of words, finds tokens of words and executes the tokens in left to right order.

- Forth has a compiler, which compiles new words to replace lists of tokens.

- Tokens are often nested token lists. A return stack is thus required to nest and unnest token lists.

- Forth words pass numeric parameters implicitly on a first-in-last-out data stack or parameter stack, thus greatly simplify the language syntax.

In many Forth systems, a token is an address of executable code. However, a token can take other forms depending on implementation.

Text Interpreter

Forth text interpreter processes a list of words:

```
< list of words >
```

A list of words is a sequence of Forth commands names, separated by blanks or white spaces and terminated by a carriage return. Processing, or interpreting, a list words means that a name is parsed off the list, the corresponding token of the command is looked up in dictionary, and the token is executed. This process is repeated until all words are processed. Then Forth computer waits for you to type in another list of words, and process them. The mechanism in a Forth computer processing list of words, or lines of text, is called a text interpreter. The mechanism which executes a token is called an inner interpreter.

Number of commands in a word list is not limited. A list may be in one line of text, or in a huge text file.

Different types of Forth words have different inner interpreters. For code words, the code interpreter simply jumps to the machine instruction routine contained in a code word and let the underlying CPU executing these machine instructions. For colon words, an address interpreter interprets, executes, or processing the token list contained in the colon word. Because in most Forth implementations, tokens are addresses pointing to executable code, colon interpreter is often called address interpreter.

Forth text interpreter operates in two modes: interpreting mode and compiling mode. In interpreting mode, a list of words is interpreted; i.e., words are parsed and executed. In compiling mode, a list of words is compiled; i.e., words are parsed and corresponding tokens are compiled into a token list. This token list is given a name to become a new word added to the dictionary.

The most important task of text interpreter in compiling mode is to construct new colon words. Hence it is called colon compiler. In compiling new colon words, colon compiler converts word lists into equivalent token lists. It builds nested token lists one on top of the other, until a final solution is reached in the last word.

Colon Compiler

This is the most powerful feature of Forth, in that you can compile new colon words to replace lists of existing words. The syntax to define a new colon word is:

```
:  <name>  <list of existing words>  ;
```

Nested token lists are added until the final colon word becomes the solution to your problem. Words are built and tested easily from bottom up, one at a time. The solution space can be explored wider and farther, and an optimized solution can be found more quickly. Program correctness can only be proven in this bottom-up list building process.

A token list generally contains a linear sequence of address tokens. However, other data and information can be embedded in a token list to enhance its functionality. Most common embedded data are in the forms of integer literals, string literals and address literals.

Integer, Address, and String Literals

Text interpreter accepts numbers in a word list. Numbers are ASCII strings with valid numeric digits with an optional leading '-' minus sign. Text interpreter pushes an integer number on the data stack. Colon compiler compiles numbers into token lists as integer literals. An integer literal begins with an integer token followed by an integer value. Later, when the token list is interpreted, the integer literal pushes the integer back on data stack.

Colon compiler may compile string literals into lists. A string literal contains a string token followed by a string. A string is a sequence of ASCII characters terminated by a terminating character specified by the preceding string command. When the list is interpreted, the string token uses the compiled string for whatever purpose designed, and then passes control to the next token after the compiled string.

Lists are normally processed in consecutive sequence. However, branches and loops are allowed, using address literals. An address literal is like an integer literal. It begins with an address token, followed by an address. Later, when a token list is interpreted, the address token causes a conditional or unconditional branch to the following address. Branches and loops are constructed with address literals.

String literals and integer literals insert data into token lists, but do not alter execution sequence. Address literals change sequential flow in lists. Forth uses special control structure commands to construct control structures, which are sub-lists having only one entry point and one exit point. There might be branches and loops within a control structure, but it is not allowed to have more than one entry and on exit. Control structures can be nested, but cannot overlap each other.

A control structure, or simply a structure, is a sub-list of tokens within which execution sequence can be modified dynamically. The following figure shows a sequential structure, a branch structure and a loop structure:

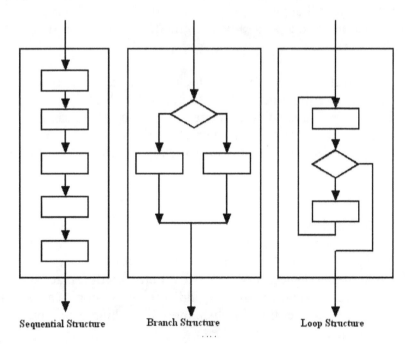

Sequential Structure   Branch Structure   Loop Structure

A structure has only one entry point and one exit point, although it may have many branches inside. Structures can be nested, but may not overlap. A structure can therefore be considered an enhanced token. A colon word is then a structure given a name.

Using the concept of structures, a new colon word has the following syntax:

```
:   <name>   <list of structures>   ;
```

Data Stack and Return Stack

The fundamental reason why word lists (command lists or token lists) in Forth can be simple, linear sequences of commands is that Forth uses two stacks: a return stack to store nested return addresses, and a data stack to pass parameters among nested commands. Parameters are passed implicitly on the data stack, and do not have to be explicitly invoked. Therefore, Forth commands can be interpreted in a linear sequence, and tokens can be stored in simple, linear token lists. Language syntax is greatly simplified, internal representation of code is greatly simplified, and execution speed is greatly increased.

It is an interesting point of view to look at Forth as a list processor. I have not seen a formal proof that lists can solve all computable problems. But, I have yet to encounter a problem which cannot be solved by Forth as nested lists. In practice, the solution to any problem in the form of nested lists generally is the most compact and most efficient.

English Analogue

Returning to the English language analogue, Forth language is a collection of commands, or words. Most Forth words replace lists of existing words, and new words are added freely. It mimics a natural language even simpler than English, more like Chinese, without complicated and artificial syntax rules. It mimics how we humans think, reason, and communicate, in the simplest fashion. It is natural intelligence, much superior to any scheme contrived as artificial intelligence. It is also the simplest way we can impart our intelligence into computers, microcontrollers, and other intelligent machines.

Virtual and Real Forth Engines

Another interesting view on Forth is from computer architectural designs. Chuck Moore explored many different ways in designing real Forth computers. Instead of designing a Virtual Forth Engine superposed on a real computer, he proved that it was possible to build Real Forth Engine with current semiconductor technology. Most of the primitive code words required in a Virtual Forth Engine could be implemented in semiconductor circuits. The return stack and data stack could also be implemented in hardware, and thus eliminated the memory bottleneck in stack operations in conventional computer architectures.

Conceptually, the best computer design for a particular application is the one in which all required instructions are implemented in hardware. This kind of dedicated special purpose computer is economically prohibitive, and cannot be built physically. A feasible alternative is to build a general purpose computer with a limited set of instructions implemented in hardware, and commit a host of applications in software. This is how our computer industry developed. Software grows to fill all available memory space, no matter how big it is.

Forth, on the other hand, provides us with a better and entirely feasible approach to the best, special purpose computer. We realized that it is impossible to build a Real Forth Engine with all necessary instructions in hardware, or in code words. However, it is possible to extend the Virtual Forth Engine, in adding unlimited new instructions as colon words. As far as the user is concerned, colon words behave no different than code words, only a bit slower. However, colon words can provide ALL functionality required by your application. If the computer is fast enough, your problem is solved. Otherwise, wait for a faster computer. Or, optimize your code further.

It is incredible that a simple colon compiler which turns a simple word list into a token list, and gives it a name to form a new compound command, has the unlimited power to solve problems of any complexity. But, this is what Forth is. This is what Zen is about.

Tao and Name

The most interesting aspect of Forth as a programming is that it retains names of commands in memory. In most other programming languages, names of procedures and data structures are thrown away after program is compiled. Names were only temporary devices used for the convenience of programmers in the process of programming, and they are of no value in the final product.

In a living and growing Forth system, just like natural languages, names encapsulate intelligence and are essential for thinking, reasoning, abstraction, communication, and accumulation of knowledge. Names are very important as external representations of commands, just like compiled code as internal representations of commands. When commands and data structures are given meaningful and carefully chosen names, Forth program reads like poetry, only without rhyme. Chuck Moore recommended that word lists being limited to 7 words, for ease of reading and for optimization. It would make Forth programs look like Tang poems.

Lao-Tzu (6th-5th century BC) was the first person realized the significance of names along with Tao. He had very deep understanding of nature, and perhaps, computers. He opened his Tao-Te Ching with some profound statements. Nobody really knows what he's talking about, but I do, because I think he was talking about computers. I will show you my translation and my interpretation. The Chinese text was based on a recently (1973) excavated version of Tao-Te Ching, similar to but not the same as you find in your local library.

道可道也，非恆道也。
名可名也，非恆名也。
無名萬物之始也；
有名萬物之母也。

故恆無欲也，以觀其眇；
恆有欲也，以觀其所噭。
兩者同出，異名同胃，
玄之有玄，眾眇之門。

Eternal Tao cannot be spoken,
Eternal name cannot be named.
In the beginning, Tao has no name,
But, Name is the mother of
everything.
Tao is manifested by its actions,
Name reveals the nature of Tao.
Tao and Name are one and same,
Uttermost profound, mystery of
mysteries!

Lao-Tzu was talking about Tao and Name. Tao as Nature and truth, can be observed. To understand Tao, and to communicate Tao, you need Names. I think he was actually talking about computers and firmware engineering. A computer has two components: hardware and programs. Combined, they can do wonderful things beyond human comprehension. Programs are best modularized and constructed in nested lists. If all modules and lists are given proper names, programs can be constructed, debugged, understood, and used most efficiently by human.

It is then very obvious in Forth each command has a name field and
a code field. Tao is the executable code in the code field, and Name
is in the name field. Tao do things, and Name entails relationship,
knowledge, understanding, and abstraction. Human intelligence is
based on names, or words. Words are built on other words. We think
with words. We communicate with words. We express deeply
convoluted ideas with words. Modern sciences and engineering use
many other symbols and drawing when words are not sufficient, but
computer sciences and software engineering use plain words.
Software engineers throw away the words they used to build
executable code, because these words are not needed in the end
products. Users do not need knowledge on how the product was
constructed. However, if you are a user of your program, you want
to keep the names as long as you are using it. You might have to go
back to some words to find bugs if the program had trouble. Were
the words properly preserved in the product, you would have a much
easier time to find bugs and fix them.

This is what Forth is. Names are preserved with Tao. Replacing a list
of words with a new word is how natural languages develop, how
they are used, and how they are evolving. Forth is therefore natural
intelligence, not merely artificial intelligence. You think in this way.
Why not program in the same way? You want to keep the names in
your system as long as you have ownership. You can always strip
the names out later, if you are concerned your intellectual properties.

道與名. Tao and Name. Commands with names.

That's Forth. Tao of computers.

Chapter 3. - eForth Model

eForth is a series of Forth implementations based on a very small and simple model developed in the Silicon Valley Chapter of the Forth Interest Group, in the San Francisco area. Many people inside this chapter and all over the world had made significant contributions to it. The first model was released in 1990. As it stands now, there are 14 different implementations of this model on various microprocessors, including 8086, 80386, Z80, 8096/98, 8051, 68000, 68332, 68HC11, PIC17C42, Transputer, and the experimental P21.

The basic model used the direct-thread model to implement the inner interpreter, but there are several versions of subroutine threaded code around. The basic model used the Microsoft MASM as the software platform, but there are many versions using the native assemblers of the targeted microprocessor. The basic model came with a minimum set of utilities, but there are several versions highly optimized and with lots of utilities.

With eForth we hoped to achieve two goals: one is to encourage people who do not have any prior Forth experience to learn Forth and evaluate it for possible applications. The other was to enable experienced Forth programmer to port this model to newer and more powerful microprocessors. It seems that we have made good progress in both directions.

It is amazing that eForth had gained that much ground without a detailed and complete documentation. I hope that by going through the source code of the 8086 implementation line by line in this book, users can understand this system better and can make better use of this model in their applications.

Origin of eForth

eForth is the name of a Forth model designed to be simple so that it can be easily understood by programmers with some elementary knowledge about assembly languages. It ought to be easily portable to a large number of newer and more powerful processors which are available now and are becoming available in the near future. Originally it was called pigForth. However, because of very strong objections among many experienced Forth programmers, a less provocative name 'eForth' was adopted after much heated debates at a beer party in the 1990 Rochester Forth Conference, held in June 1990, Rochester, New York.

PIG originally stood for Post-Forth Interest Group, a term used by Mr. Andreas Gopold, a Forth programmer from Germany, to encourage people to think the future of Forth, in light of the recent advancements in computer hardware and software technologies. His feeling was that Forth in its present shape and form will not be useful for the programmers in the future, because it does not provide enough support for program development, especially for large and very demanding projects. He thus felt that Forth has to develop in the direction as Tom Zimmer's FPC, Mitch Bradley's ForthMacs, and Leibnitz he developed. These systems are huge because they incorporate lots of tools and utilities useful in the programming.

I stole this acronym 'pig' from him for a different purpose. As we were marching into the nineties, confronting a host of new and very powerful microprocessors of different architecture and designs. The excitement was not the least less intense than that in the seventies when the first crop of 8 bit microprocessors made their appearance. Forth Interest Group captured the imagination of the first generation of personal computer users by releasing the figForth model riding on six different microprocessors. It was thus very interesting to see if we could build a new Forth which can be easily ported to many, if not all, of the new and future microprocessors. This is the original design goal of eForth.

eForth Model

eForth model defined a minimal Forth system which turned a computer into a Virtual Forth Engine (VFE) on which users could build applications and to test the applications interactively. At the topmost layer, an outer (text) interpreter accepts words from you and executes them. In this layer, a rich set of utility words are available to allow you to compile new words into the dictionary, decompile words in the dictionary, inspect and change memory, inspect and change data stack, and download files through a terminal device. These are functions a normal operating system provides. In eForth, these functions are provided in one simple, elegant, and integrated program.

At the lowest layer, the eForth was built upon 31 primitive words which had to be coded in native machine instructions. This set of primitive words was selected for portability, because we intended that the eForth model to be implemented on many different computers. Ideally, one could port eForth to a new computer by recoding only this set of primitive words, and the rest of the system could be ported over unmodified. This portability had been proven in many cases, although there were cases where we had to make minor changes to port it to a computer with strange architecture.

This set of primitive words imposes the Virtual Forth Engine on a real life computer and make it behave like an idealized Forth computer, with two stacks and a dictionary. By limiting the number of machine specific primitive words, we also impose a performance penalty on eForth, which does not take advantages of the resources designed into a real computer. However, it is expected that the user will improve its performance by replacing the most often used high level words with low level code words.

Changing Environment

In the seventies, personal computers were novelties, totally stand-alone systems that you had on your desk, and they worked for you. Or, more precisely, you willingly became enslaved to them. A personal computer, however, had to contain a programming environment to be useful. Thus one needed a CPU with memory, a keyboard, a display monitor, one or more disk drives, and an operating system including programming languages and utilities. A personal computer had to be self-sufficient and stand-alone.

figForth was originally written by William Ragsdale for an Apple II computer. Bill organized the Forth Interest Group in 1978. Among the first things he did was gathering a group of programmers to port it to other personal computers popular at the time.

figForth, as all other Forth systems at that time, had to be self-sufficient also. It had to be able to support the keyboard input, screen and printer output, and disk drives for mass storage. An editor was always the first application a Forth user wrote, because that was the only way he could proceed to do serious programming.

figForth was adopted in many commercial Forth systems, which generally added an editor, an assembler, and some demonstration programs. It was enthusiastically accepted because it was the only high level language beside BASIC which could conformably reside in 16 Kbytes of RAM memory.

F83 was developed by Henry Laxen and Michael Perry in the early 1980's. It was a giant step forward from figForth, and much human engineering went into it to facilitate programming. It included a much better editor, more extensive debugging tools, and smoother interface to operating systems. Nevertheless, F83 was still an environment to itself, tailored to a single user using a single machine.

The largest change in the eighties was the separation of the processor from the programming environment, due to proliferation of standard personal computers; i. e., IBM-PC and the clones. PC's become the default programming tool for other microprocessors in separated boxes. I do not deny that there are still lots of programming done on the PC's, for the PC's. However, a very large portion of the programming activities for newer and more advanced processors are carried out on PC's separated from the target computers.

Separating programming environment from target microprocessors had a great
impact on the design of eForth, which I presumed would go into target processors, not the host computer. It was also of great advantage to the design of eForth, because eForth did not have to include utilities used in host computer, and the eForth design requirements could be greatly simplified. At the time, more and more microprocessors developed into microcontrollers, with integrated memory and IO devices. In a sense, eForth was addressing the needs of microcontrollers, while embedded systems became the latest buzz word in the microprocessor industry.

Universal Microcontroller

The microcomputer for which figForth was designed can be shown schematically here. It contained a CPU, some memory, and it had to talk to a keyboard, a monitor, and a disk.

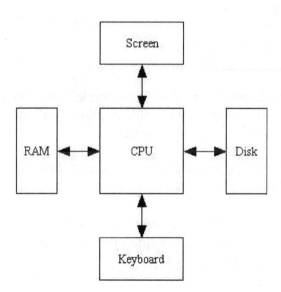

The microcontroller eForth had to deal with was much simpler, as shown in the following. It had a CPU with some memory, perhaps with many different peripheral. It was connected to the outside world through a RS232 cable. This RS232 line might not be used in actual applications, but it could be connected to a host computer for programming, testing and debugging. In certain applications, the RS232 umbilical cord might never be severed because then the host could update firmware in the target. Many of the new generation of instruments were designed using this capability.

Universal Forth

As we had defined a Universal Microcontroller, it was logical that we could define and build a Universal Forth for it. There were many trade-offs to be considered in designing this Universal Forth, which we assumed would be ported to many different microcontrollers. There were also many models of Forth we could use, taking advantages of the wisdom accumulated over the last twenty years in the Forth community.

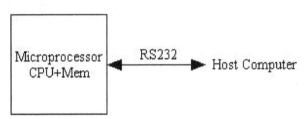

There were three most important Forth models from which eForth derived its strength: figForth by Bill Ragsdale, cmForth by Chuck Moore, and the bForth by Bill Muench.

Here is a list of important features we liked to include in this Universal Forth:

- A small set of kernel words, which is machine dependent. Only this set of words must be rewritten for a specific CPU. A minimum kernel word set encourages the porting of eForth to newer CPU's.

- High level words would be portable to all target CPU's, including 8, 16, and 32 bit machines.

- The only I/O words are KEY, EMIT, and ?KEY, because the only I/O device we need in the target is the RS232 port.

- Editor, file server, and other utilities are provided in the host system. Forth does not have to provide these services.

- Assume that the host is a PC/MS-DOS system which is the lowest cost, and the most available platform for programming.

- Source code is provided in the MASM assembly to avoid problems in metacompilation.

The guiding principles for this Forth were easy to understand, easy to modify, and easy to port to other microcontrollers. The letter 'e' in eForth thus stands for easy, educational, embedded, elegant, and perhaps, evangelical.

DOS Implementation

The ideal of eForth was discussed extensively in the Silicon Valley FIG Chapter in the period of 1990-91. Various models were evaluated to decide which one was the best for its implementation. The available models considered including figForth, F83, cmForth, LaForth, ZenForth, Fcode, ANS Standard Forth, and bForth. The consensus favored bForth, whose principal author was Bill Muench. It had a very small core of machine specific word set, and had the most of the features desired in eForth. Bill distributed a preliminary specification based on bForth for the group to work on. I took the model and implemented it on an IBM-PC, in MASM assembly. This implementation formed the basis of the eForth Model.

The eForth Model is targeted to Intel 8086 processors under DOS environment. It relied on DOS to provide the serial I/O services. It was a fully functional Forth system which allowed a user to exercise it and evaluated its word set.

Following are some of the special features in the original eForth Model:

- 31 machine dependent code words and 193 high level colon words.

- Direct Threaded Code.

- Separated name and code dictionaries.

- All system variables are defined as user variables for ROMmability.

- Vectored ?KEY, KEY, and EMIT.

- File handling through the serial I/O interface.

- CATCH-THROW error handler.

- Only the single indexed FOR-NEXT loop is provided.

- Track the proposed ANS Forth Standard.

- Compile-only words are trapped in interpretive mode.

- Tools include DUMP, WORDS, SEE and .S .

- Flexibility in memory mapping.

Porting eForth

The eForth Model was designed for portability and every effort was made to facilitate the porting process. The eForth system was relative small wherein the code dictionary was 5 Kbytes long and the name dictionary was 2 Kbytes long. The following procedure is suggested for porting it to a new CPU:

- Determine the memory map in target system. Set the memory pointers in the EQU section properly to reflect physical memory assignments in target system; i.e., ROM, RAM, stacks, user area, code dictionary and name dictionary.

- Study code words in the machine dependent kernel. Rewrite them in assembly for the target CPU. If you have access to an assembler of the target CPU, use it to assemble this set of code words. If you do not have an assembler, hand assemble the code words using MASM. It seems difficult to do hand assembly, but you have only 31 words to worry about.

- If you have tools to exercise the assembly code words, try to debug them.

- The binary object from the assembler has to be entered into the eForth source code

- using DB and DW directives, which can be handled by MASM.

- Assemble eForth source code by MASM to produce a binary object code.

- Move the binary object code into your target system via EPROM's or other means.

- Debug the target system.

The eForth Model assumed that the CPU addressed bytes in memory. All memory accessing words use byte addresses. If your CPU could not address bytes, you have to synthesize a byte addressing space from the cell addressing space, and provide a mechanism to translate byte addresses into cell addresses and vice versa. The eForth Model does enforce words alignment to cell boundaries to facilitate byte-to-cell address translation.

Hand assembling machine code was not the most pleasant task in programming. However, it was impossible to provide the eForth Model in all the assembler formats used by all the CPU manufacturers. Adopting MASM as the common source code assembly environment established the largest common denominator for porting eForth to the largest number of CPU's.

After the generic eForth Model is ported to a target CPU, you might want to consider optimizing it to improve its performance. Following is a list of words which are primary candidates to be re-coded in machine instructions:

- Recode +, -, UM* and UM/MOD if you want to do number crunching.

- Recode (PARSE) and NUMBER? to speed up interpretation and compilation.

- Recode doUSER and doVAR. Use CALL doUSE and CALL doVAR to replace the high level mechanisms in the eForth Model.

- Recode FIND to improve the dictionary searching.

- Add ONLY-ALSO mechanism to use multiple vocabularies.

eForth1 Implementations

After 86eForth v1.0 was released in 1990, many Forth programmers port it to their favorite microprocessors. Implementations received included these microprocessors:

8086 eForth Model, Bill Muench and C. H. Ting, 1990
A small portable Forth system designed for microprocessors of the 90's. 31 machine dependent kernel words and 191 high level words. Separated code and name dictionaries. Source code is in Microsoft MASM assembly. Disk and eForth Implementation Guide.

8051 eForth, C. H. Ting, 1990
A small ROM based Forth system for the popular Intel 8051/31 microcontroller. Source code is in Microsoft MASM assembly. Easily modifiable to suit specific ROM/RAM configurations. Source code on an IBM 5.25" disk. With 8051 eForth Implementation Note.

68000 eForth, Richard H. Haskell, 1990
A 32-bit 68000 implementation of eForth for the Motorola ECB Board. Dr. Ting also contributed a file in that MASM is forced to produce code in the Motorola byte order.

32-Bit 8086 eForth, Rick VanNorman, 1990
This is a 32 bit implementation of eForth for 80x8x family of processors. Much of the high level code are rewritten in assembly to improve the performance. The object code is generated by a Forth metacompiler (included), not from MASM source. Many other utilities are provided and are good eForth coding examples.

Transputer eForth, Bob Barr, 1990
eForth for Inmos 32-bit transputers. This is an experimental implementation not yet tested on a Transputer system. Volunteers are welcome to put this system to the test.

Z80 eForth, Ken Chen, 1991
Ken Chen is a member of Taiwan FIG Chapter. He moved eForth to the popular Z80 processor with significant enhancement. It also contains a diagnostic program for eForth which allows the implementor to debug eForth during cold boot.

Subroutine Threaded eForth, R. H. Haskell, 1991
Dr. Haskell recoded eForth using subroutine threading so that all high level words can be executed and tested as coded words. This disk includes 68000, 68HC11 and 8086 implementations with a host interface in F-PC.

68HC11 eForth, Karl Lunt, 1991
This eForth is based on a public domain 68HC11 assembler ASM11. The native assembler makes it easier for the user to extend the eForth and optimize the kernel for specific applications.

8098/96 eForth, Kezhong Ting, 1991
This eForth for the Intel 8098/96 family of microcontroller is contributed by an author from Nanjing, People's Republic of China. Also includes a 8096 assembler written in FPC.

Pic17C42 eForth, C. H. Ting, 1993
eForth for Microchip's 16-bit high performance microcontroller. Written in ASM17 assembler.

8051 and 68HC11 eForth, W. Schemmert, 1993
Opitmized eForth for 8051 and 68HC11, written in native UCASM assemblers. Most of the documentation is in German. Supplied with EFTERM terminal emulator.

386 eForth on DPMI, Rick VanNorman, 1993
This eForth runs under Windows through the DPMI interface. 32-bit registers and addressing space in the protected mode.

MIPS eForth, C. H. Ting, 1993
eForth implemented for MIPS microprocessors in Silicon Graphics Workstation. Use a small C loader and call I/O routines in C library.

H8 eForth, Bernie Mentink, 1993
Mentink of New Zealand contributed this eForth for H8/532 from Hitachi. H8 is very powerful. It has on-chip counter/timers, 3 PWM, 10-bit A/D, 65 I/O pins, 1Kb ram 32 Kb OTP ROM, 20 MHz crystal.

7810 eForth, John Talbert, 1994
John Talbert at Oberlin Observatory contributed this for NEC78C10. 7810 has 3 8-bit I/O ports, 8-bit A/d, serial I/O, 256 bytes of RAM and 10 16-bit registers. Another powerful Japanese microcontroller.

56002 eForth, Dave Taliaferro, 1996
First working version of eForth for Motorola 56002 DSP chip. Include Motorola 56000 Assembler and the assembler manual.

68HC16 eForth, Pete Zawasky, 1996
A direct threaded eForth assembled with Motorola ToolWare M68HC16 Assembler and used on M68HC16EVB board.

Java eForth, Michael Losh, 1997
Java implementation of eForth for Java Virtual Machine. Token threaded, word addressing, accessed through a console-style Java applet. Opened in a browser like Netscape Navigator and Microsoft Internet Explorer.

PowePC eForth, C. H. Ting, 1998
A tool program running under MPW on PowerPC Macintosh. NEXT is a branch-through-link-register machine instruction and the Forth virtual engine is very fast.

6805 eForth Version 1.03, C. H. Ting, 1998
Subroutine threaded eForth is ported to 6805. Fully optimized so that the interpreter and compiler run as fast as possible.

eForth2 Implementations

In the subsequent years, I tried to optimize eForth for several microcontrollers for industrial applications. I started experimenting with subroutine thread model, and called these implementations eForth2. All earlier implementations were thus called eForth1. The eForth2 implementations were:

8051eForth Version 2.03, 1998
Enhanced eForth for 8051. Optimized using subroutine threading. Name and code dictionary unified. It can load source code and dump core image through the serial port. It is useful to develop substantial applications.

68HC12eF for 68HC12, 2000
Optimzed eForth system for 68HC11/12 microcontroller. Simplified according to 8086 eForth v 2.02. Subroutine threading. Reduced

system variables. Combined name and code dictionary. Great for motor and instrumental control.

2181eF for Analog Devices AD2181 DSP, 2000
This eForth is to be installed in a 1MB EPROM plugged into the Analog Devices EZKIT-Lite, ADSP2181 EZ-LAB board. This board communicates with the PC through HyperTerminal, which allows you to do DSP experiments interactively.

eForthXA for Philips 80C51XA, 1998
80C51XA is a 16-bit clone of 8051 from Phillips. It has an interesting machine instruction JMP[[IP+]] which is $NEXT in eForth. It is almost a native Forth microcontroller. I used this eForth to drive a robotic arm. Extremely powerful.

ADuCeForth for Analog Devices ADuC702x, 2005
Based on an Analog Devices' ADuC7020, which includes a 32-bit ARM7 microcontroller and a host of peripheral devices, including ADC, DAC, 8 KB RAM and 92 KB flash. eForth is downloaded to flash through an UART port. It is an excellent platform using Forth to develop real time industrial applications.

SAM7eF for Atmel AT91SAM7X256, 2008
This eForth system runs on an Olimax development board with a 132x132 color LCD display. AT91SAM7 is an ARM7 microcontroller with 256 KB of flash and 64 KB of RAM, from Atmel. eForth boots from flash and copies itself to RAM and run from it. It is the first microcontroller for eForth that you don't have to worry about memory.

CeForth Versions 1.0/1.1, 2009
The two version of eForth are written in C. They are compiled by gcc in Cygwin. V1.0 has 33 primitives. V1.It has 64 primitives, and are much faster than V1.0. eForth dictionary is a big data structure generated externally by a F# metacompiler and copied into C code. They are targeted to C programmers who are curious abort Forth language.

STM8eForth for STM8S Discovery, 2010
STM8S is an 8 bit microcontroller from STMicroelectronics, distributing on a STM8S-Discovery Board for less than $10. STM8S105C6 chip has 32 Kbytes of flash memory and 2 Kbytes of RAM memory. eForth core is stored in and executed from flash memory. New Forth words are added to RAM memory.

eF32q for eP32 Chip, 2010
eP32 is a 32 bit microcontroller implemented for FPGA chip LatticeXP2-5E-6TN144C on its Brevia Development Kit at $49. eForth system incorporated on eP32 for chip validation and testing. ef32q is produced by a metacompiler written in F#, based on 27 primitive machine instructions.

328eForth for Arduino Uno Kit, 2011
Arduino Uno is a wonderful kit for DIY hobbyists. It integrates an ATmega328P microcontroller from Atmel with 32 KB of flash and 2 KB of RAM. It connects to a PC through USB and is a complement development system. 328eForth can be extended directly in flash memory and makes it very easy to develop substantial applications. ATmega328P is still in a 28-pin DIP package!

eF16R for eP16 Chip, 2012
eP16 is a 16 bit microcontroller implemented for FPGA chip LatticeXP2-5E-6TN144C on its Brevia Development Kit at $49. eForth system incorporated on eP16 for chip validation and testing. ef16R is produced by a metacompiler written in F#, based on 30 primitive machine instructions.

430eForth for TI LaunchPad, 2012
This is a Forth system for the MSP430G2553 microcontroller used on LaunchPad kit from TI, $4.30 initially. It is a 16-bit Forth assembled on Code Composer Studio 5.2. It makes the best used of the 16 KB of flash memory, leaving about 10 KB for your applications. The inner interpreter $NEXT is reduced to a single MSP430G2 instruction mov @ip+,pc.

STM32eForth720 for STM32 F4 Discovery, 2014

This eForth is for STM32F407 chip on STM32 F4 Discovery Kit from STMicroelectronics. This chip has 1 MB flash memory, 192 KB of RAM, and a ton of interesting IO devices. It is no longer an ARM7 chip, but a THUMB2 chip. STMeForth720 is optimized for the new environment.

80eForth202 for eP8080 Chip, 2016

eP8080 was a model used in SVFIG FPGA Design Workshop. It recreated i8080 chip in FPGA. 80eForth202 is the eForth system embedded in VHDL design to validate the chip design and to help debugging the chip. It is derived from 86eForth V2.2 and Z80eForth by Ken Chen, and is assembled with MASM.

PDP1eForth for ePDP1 Chip, 2016

ePDP1 was another model used in SVFIG FPGA Design Workshop. It recreated PDP1 chip in FPGA. PDP1eForth is the eForth system embedded in VHDL design to validate the chip design and to help debugging the chip. It is derived from eP16, and used a metacompiler in F# to create a eForth dictionary to initialize RAM memory.

More recently, I used VHDL to design Forth processors and tried them on FPGA's. They include a 16-bit processor P16 and a 32-bit processor eP32. I ported eForth to these chips for testing and verification. This year (2016), we had a CPU Design Workshop in Silicon Valley Forth Interest Group, and I used Intel 8080 processor and DEC PDP1processor as exercises. I also ported eForth to these historical processors for testing and verification. It is interesting that eForth was used here instead of the traditional test benches, which were much more difficult to design and implement for chip testing and verification.

Evolution of 86eForth

Initially, I was very happy with 86eForth v1.0, as it ran on a fairly advanced 16-bit microprocessor at the time. Architecture-wise, the 16-bit 8086 was much inferior to the 32-bit 68000, but the Intel-IBM-Microsoft branding started to dominate the PC industry by evolving 8086 to 80186, 80286, and to 80386. It was painful for Intel to bridge the gap between a 16-bit architecture to a 32-bit architecture, and we all suffered with it. Following were attempts to move eForth into 32-bit protected moode:

8086 eForth Version 2.02, 1999
Enhanced eForth for 8086. Name and code dictionary unified. It can load source code from DOS text files and dump EXE file image. It is useful to develop substantial applications in the DOS environment.

16-Bit 386 eForth, V 3.01, C. H. Ting, 1991
This is a 16 bit implementation of eForth for 80386 in the protected mode. It came with Al Williams' DOS extender and calls DOS keyboard and screen services.

32-Bit 386 eForth V.4.02, C. H. Ting, 1996
This is a 32 bit implementation of eForth for 80386 in the protected mode. It enters into protected mode directly under DOS through an OK loader provided by Chuck Moore. Only COM1 is active at 9600 baud. Keyboard, screen and disks are all silenced. You need another PC to serve as a host through the serial port.

32-Bit 386 eForth V.4.03, C. H. Ting, 1996
This is a 32 bit implementation of eForth for 80386 in the protected mode. It replaces the Video BIOS at C0000H and is activated by system BIOS. It converts a 386/486 motherboard to a diskless, embedded Forth processor, communicating with a PC through the COM1 port.

I tried to jump to the 32-bit protected mode in 86eForth v3.1 and up to v4.3. Switching back to real mode to perform IO operations was not pleasant. Finally, I realized that PC was a Windowed and networked mainframe computer. Trying to run it like an embedded system was futile. It was more fun to work with other microcontrollers which were getting faster, bigger, and more capable in their IO functions.

However, a young fellow, Chien-shin Yep, in Taiwan Forth Interest Group took 86eForth v4.3 and integrated it into the Windows environment. He released it as F# in 2002, which had a nice console window, and could invoke all Windows API. It was a very pleasant Forth system to use, and I wrote many interesting applications with it. I could open a canvas window and draw shapes and text in it. I could also produce MIDI files, and then moved all my Bach organ pieces to MIDI.

F#, Cheah-shen Yap, 2002
eForth for Windows XP. Yap put in hooks to access Windows API, and thus allows us to develop applications for Windows. It used an .FEX file to organize source code files, and very large applications could be developed easily.

Another thread in the evolution of eForth was to simplify it for microcontrollers. There were lots of functions in 86eForth v1.0 which had never been used in embedded applications, like multitasking and CATCH-THROW error handler. Separated name and code dictionary added extra complexity to the system architecture. I planned to remove them in 86eForth v2.0, to lead of eForth2, but did not find time to actually do it until 1999, and that was 86eForth v2.2.

PC has changed a lot since 1999. It marched from 32-bit to 64-bit. Windows also marched from Windows 3 to Windows 10. Recently, thinking of revising this book, I retrieved 86eForth v2.2 and tried to assemble it. I found a copy of MASM 6.1, and assembled it successfully. However, the .exe file could only be executed under Windows XP, not even under Windows 7, which politely complained that the 32-bit system could not handle old 16-bit programs.

I thought that this book will be useless if I could not provide a working .exe file under the current Windows systems. Microsoft no longer supports MASM. It recently released Visual Studio 2016 Community, and touted it as the ultimate IDE for software development for Windows and other computing platforms. It supports Visual Basic, Visual C++, C#, JavaScript, Python, and Visual F# (not my F#). After much searching on Google, I found that MASM is now buried under Visual C++, and Kip Irvine gave very detailed instructions on how to activate the assembler. Kip wrote a book *Assembly Language for x86 Processors,* which was very helpful for me to get re-acquainted with 80x86 instruction set.

I cleaned up 86eForth v2.2 to become 86eForth v2.3, and combined it with 86eForth v4.3for a 32-bit eForth running under Visual Studio 2015 Community.

32-Bit 386 eForth V.5.2 for Visual Studio, C. H. Ting, 2016
It is a sole assembly file in a C++ console project. It requires include and library files supplied by Kip Irvine for Windows services. It uses indirect thread model so that new colon words can be added to the .data segment. It is optimized with 71 code words and 110 colon words.

Following Kip's instructions, I was able to combine 86eForth v2.2 and v4.3 to build a new version of eForth, which is 32-bit and working in a DOS like console windows. 86eForth v5.1 was still using direct thread model and could not be extended, because I could not add new words to the .code segment. In 86eForth v5.2, I changed to indirect thread model, and can now add new Forth words to the .data segment.

I am now using 86eForth v5.2 as the basis of this third edition of eForth and Zen. I will try to explain the whole system using the assembly source code, and follow it exactly in the loading order. In this way, I hope you can understand this system without any prior knowledge of Forth. What you need are familiarity with MASM and 80x86 instruction set, and an open mind to see how Forth interpreter and compiler are constructed. What you learn from these discussions might not be very useful in the Windows environment, but very important when you try to program embedded systems, where you cannot rely on an operating system to manage the CPU, memory, and IO devices for you.

Chapter 4. - Assemble eForth on Visual Studio

The purpose of eForth is to show you how a simple Forth can be implemented and tested on a microcontroller of your choice. The original 86eForth v1.0 was constructed as a model to help you understand Forth and implement it yourself. It was first release in 1990 on a PC with 8086/88 CPU under Microsoft DOS with MASM assembler. DOS and MASM are not readily available now, and Windows and Visual Studio are the most convenient tools you have easy access. 86eForth v5.2 allows you to learn Forth and see how it is constructed at the bit level, on a modern 32-bit 80x86 CPU. Here I will tell you exactly how to install it and do some elementary experiments on it.

Visual Studio 2015 Community

When you start Visual Studio 2015 Community, you will first see this boot up screen:

After a couple of minutes, Visual Studio finishes its initialization and show you're the sign-on display:

You can start and new project, or select and prior project to run. You can read other information about Visual Studio by clicking the subjects on the right side of the display. If you click Start

Debugger

Pull down Debug menu and select Start Debugging, eForth will run
and the display changes to the following"

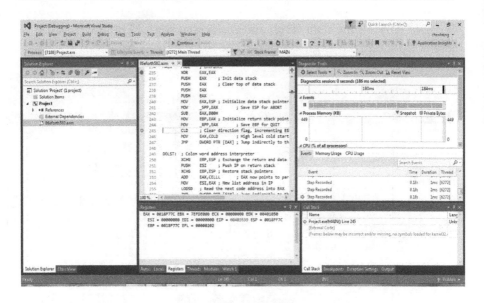

My project was set up as a Windows console project. The objective is to set u a console window like what you used to see in DOS. When eForth program starts to run, you will see it as the following:

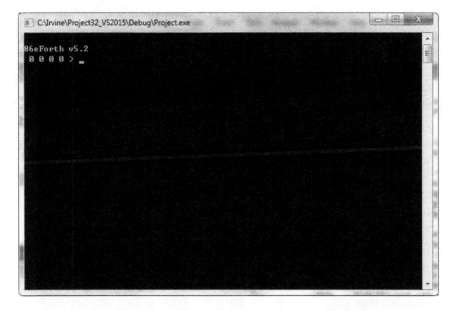

In order to show you how the debugger works, I aet up a break point at the beginning to my entry point MAIN. After breaking at MAIN, I open several windows to show the CPU registers, the memory areas around MAIN, the data stack and the return stack. These windows show how a Forth engine works. The display is as follows:

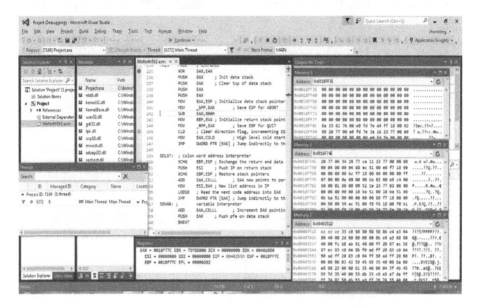

This busy display shows the power of Visual Studio as an IDE for software development. I am only interested in assembly programming, which was supported very well. I assume that it provides similar if not better support to other languages and applications. It will take lot more time and efforts to explore the possibilities.

Assembling 86eForth v5.2

MASM is now buried under Visual Studio 2015 Community Visual C++ in. Kip Irvine wrote *Assembly Language for 80x86 Processors* (7th edition, 2015) which is a nice book for 80x86 assembly programming. He also posted instructions on how to load Visual Studio 2015, and configure it to assemble assembly source code. I am outlining the steps to assemble 86eForth v5.2 and run it on Visual Studio:

1, Click the following link to show Kip's web page (might not be available or have moved):

http://kipirvine.com/asm/examples/index.htm

2. To install Kip's link libraries and example programs, click the following link
Example programs and link library source code for the Seventh Edition.
The libraries and examples are stored in a Microsoft Install (.MSI) file that installs into the **c:\Irvine** folder. Unless you have some objection to using that location, do not alter the path.

3. Google Visual Studio 2015 Community and click the following link:
https://www.visualstudio.com/en-us/products/visual-studio-community-vs.aspx
Install Visual Studio 2015 Community following instructions therein. It will take a long time. Be sure to select C++ language optional before installation.

4. If you had installed Visual Studio 2015 Community without C++ language option, add it by:
Select Tools | Import and Export Settings from the menu
Select the "Import selected environment settings" radio button
Select the "No, just import. ." radio button
Select "Visual C++" from the Default Settings List and click the Next button
Click the Finish button, then click the Close button

5. Open a project for assembly by:
Start Visual Studio.
To begin, open our sample Visual Studio project file by selecting **File/Open/Project** from the Visual Studio menu.
Navigate to your working folder where you unzipped our project file, and select the file named **Project.sln**.

6. Copy 86eForth502.asm to your working folder.

7. Add 86eForth502.asm to your project by:
Right-click the project name in the Visual Studio window, select Add, select Existing Item.

In the *Add Existing Item* dialog window, browse to the location of
86eforth502.asm, select the filename, and click the Add button to
close the dialog window.
The Solution Explorer window should look like:

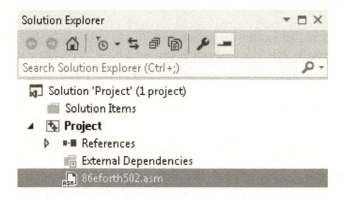

Double click 86eforth502.asm, you can open the assembly file in the
editor window:

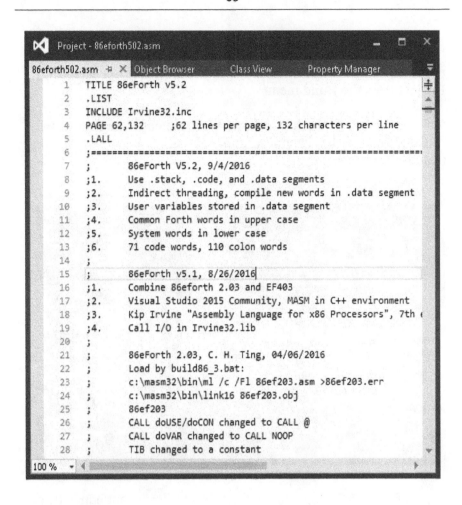

8. Click **Build Project** from the Build menu. In the Output window for Visual Studio at the bottom of the screen, you should see messages similar to the following, indicating the build progress:

If you do not see these messages, the project has probably not been modified since it was last built. No problem--just select **Rebuild Project** from the Build menu.

9. Select **Start Debugging** from the Debug menu. The following console window should appear, although your window will be larger than the one shown here:

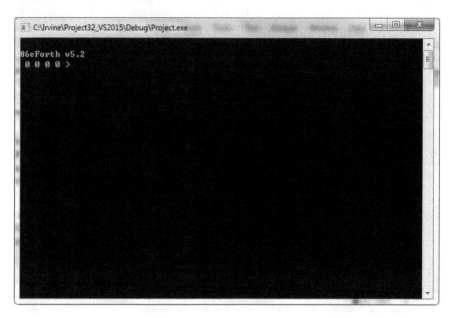

10. 86eForth v5.2 is up, and ready to accept Forth commands from you. Type

```
WORDS
: TEST CR ." HELLO, World!" ;
TEST
```
And you will see something like the following:

```
C:\Irvine\Project32_VS2015\Debug\Project.exe

86eForth v5.2
 0 0 0 0 >
 0 0 0 0 >
 0 0 0 0 > WORDS
 cold SEE WORDS .id >name .s DUMP VARIABLE CONSTANT CREATE IMMEDIATE : ] ; overt
 $compile $,n ?unique ." $" ABORT" WHILE ELSE AFT THEN REPEAT ahead IF AGAIN UNT
IL NEXT BEGIN FOR $," literal compile [compile] , ALLOT ' quit preset eval .ok [
 $interpret ?stack abort" ABORT query accept ktap tap ^h name? find same? name>
token WORD \ < .< parse (parse) ."! $"! do$ CR TYPE SPACES SPACE nuf? number? di
git? DECIMAL HEX ? . U. U.R .R str #> SIGN #S # HOLD <# extract digit pack$ ERAS
E FILL CMOVE @EXECUTE TIB PAD HERE COUNT 2@ 2! +! PICK depth >char BL 2- 2+ 1- 1
+ 4* 4- 4+ */ */MOD M* * UM* / MOD /MOD M/MOD UM/MOD WITHIN MIN MAX < U< = ABS -
 DNEGATE NEGATE NOT D+ + 2DUP 2DROP ROT ?DUP last cp context 'ev hld #tib >in sp
an tmp base rp0 sp0 UM+ XOR OR AND 0< OVER SWAP DUP DROP sp! sp@ >R R@ R> rp! rp
@ C@ C! @ ! donxt branch ?branch dolit EXIT EXECUTE EMIT KEY ?KEY BYE
 0 0 0 0 >
 0 0 0 0 > : TEST CR ." HELLO, WORLD!" ;
 0 0 0 0 > TEST
HELLO, WORLD!
 0 0 0 0 >
 0 0 0 0 > _
```

Congratulations! You have successfully assembled and run 86eForth
v5.2.

eForth Words

WORDS is a command which dumps the dictionary of eForth. It
shows the names of all Forth words assembled in the system. There
are 173 of them. I assembled all the commonly useful Forth words in
upper case, and all the infrequently used system words in lower case.
86eForth v5.2 system is case sensitive. I expect you to push the Caps
Lock key and type Forth words in upper case. If you have to use a
system word, release Caps Lock and type in lower case.

Although the system words are in lower case, in the following
discussions, I will show them in upper case, so that they stand out in
text. In several earlier eForth systems, I eliminated the header of
system words, so that they were not displayed at all by WORDS. It
was helpful in simplifying the appearance of an eForth system to
lessen apprehension of first time Forth users. These headers are

retained in 86eForth v5.2, principally because I have a colon word decompiler, which would not show the names of system words if their headers were removed.

Words in dictionary are linked backward. Therefore, the last word COLD appears first, and the first word BYE appears the last, as shown in the console window above.

In the original 86eForth v1.0, there were 31 primitive code words and 183 high level colon words. In 86eForth v5.2, there are 75 code words and 108 colon words. However, you cannot easily distinguish code words from colon words, except reading the assembly source code or examining object code in memory. Actually, a word written as code word behaves identically as if written as colon word, except it is faster and often shorter.

Dumping Memory

A very useful tool command DUMP allows you to examine different areas of memory. For example, the first word in eForth is BYE. You can get the code field address of BYE by typing:

```
` BYE
```

and its code field address shows up on the top of the data stack. Type DUMP, and you can see 128 bytes of data starting at this address. Now, the console window looks like this:

```
C:\Irvine\Project32_VS2015\Debug\Project.exe
IL NEXT BEGIN FOR $," literal compile [compile] , ALLOT ' quit preset eval .ok [
$interpret ?stack abort" ABORT query accept ktap tap ^h name? find same? name>
token WORD \ ( .( parse (parse) ."! $"! do$ CR TYPE SPACES SPACE nuf? number? di
git? DECIMAL HEX ? . U. U.R .R str #> SIGN #S # HOLD <# extract digit pack$ ERAS
E FILL CMOVE @EXECUTE TIB PAD HERE COUNT 2@ 2! +! PICK depth >char BL 2- 2+ 1- 1
+ 4* 4- 4+ */ */MOD M* * UM* / MOD /MOD M/MOD UM/MOD WITHIN MIN MAX < U< = ABS -
DNEGATE NEGATE NOT D+ + 2DUP 2DROP ROT ?DUP last cp context 'ev hld #tib >in sp
an tmp base rp0 sp0 UM+ XOR OR AND 0< OVER SWAP DUP DROP sp! sp@ >R R@ R> rp! rp
@ C@ C! @ ! donxt branch ?branch dolit EXIT EXECUTE EMIT KEY ?KEY BYE
 0 0 0 0 >
 0 0 0 0 > : TEST CR ." HELLO, WORLD!" ;
 0 0 0 0 > TEST
HELLO, WORLD!
 0 0 0 0 >
 0 0 0 0 > ' BYE
 0 0 0 403565 > DUMP
   403565  69 35 40  0 6A  0 E8  C 24  0  0 61 35 40  0  4 i5@_j_h_$__a5@__
   403575  3F 4B 45 59 7D 35 40  0 33 DB 33 C0 E8 A7 DA FF ?KEY>5@_3[3@h'Z_
   403585  FF 74  2 50 4B 53 AD FF 20 74 35 40  0  3 4B 45 _t_PKS-_ t5@__KE
   403595  59 9A 35 40  0 E8 A2 DA FF FF 83 E0 7F 50 AD FF Y_5@_h"Z___'_P-_
   4035A5  20 92 35 40  0  4 45 4D 49 54 B3 35 40  0 58 E8 __5@__EMIT35@_Xh
   4035B5  E7 DA FF FF AD FF 20 AA 35 40  0  7 45 58 45 43 gZ__-_ *5@__EXEC
   4035C5  55 54 45 CC 35 40  0 58 FF 20 C0 35 40  0  4 45 UTEL5@_X_ @5@__E
   4035D5  58 49 54 DC 35 40  0 87 EC 5E 87 EC AD FF 20 D3 XIT\5@__1^_1-_ S
 0 0 0 0 >
```

The memory is displayed in hexadecimal, and the machine instructions do not make much sense. However, looking closely, you will see the names of subsequent Forth commands: ?KEY, KEY, EMIT, EXECUTE, and EXIT. You can pick any area in the .code segment and dump the memory.

.code segment is interesting. Type

```
sp0
```

and you will see the address of this system variable as 408004. Type DUMP and the console window looks like this:

```
C:\Irvine\Project32_VS2015\Debug\Project.exe
HELLO, WORLD!
 0  0  0  >
 0  0  0  > ' BYE
 0  0  0  403565 > DUMP
    403565   69 35 40   0 6A   0 E8   C 24   0   0 61 35 40   0   4 i5@_j_h_$__a5@__
    403575   3F 4B 45 59 7D 35 40   0 33 DB 33 C0 E8 A7 DA FF ?KEY}5@_3[3@h'Z_
    403585   FF 74   2 50 4B 53 AD FF 20 74 35 40   0   3 4B 45 _t_PKS-__t5@__KE
    403595   59 9A 35 40   0 E8 A2 DA FF FF 83 E0 7F 50 AD FF Y_5@_h"Z___'_P-_
    4035A5   20 92 35 40   0   4 45 4D 49 54 B3 35 40   0 58 E8 __5@__EMIT35@_Xh
    4035B5   E7 DA FF FF AD FF 20 AA 35 40   0   7 45 58 45 43 gZ__-_ *5@__EXEC
    4035C5   55 54 45 CC 35 40   0 58 FF 20 C0 35 40   0   4 45 UTEL5@_X_ @5@__E
    4035D5   58 49 54 DC 35 40   0 87 EC 5E 87 EC AD FF 20 D3 XIT\5@__1^_1-_ S
 0  0  0  >
 0  0  0  >
 0  0  0  > sp0
 0  0  0  408004 > DUMP
    408004   7C FF 18   0 7C F7 18   0 10   0   0   0   4   0   0   0 !___|w_____
    408014    4   0   0   0   0   0   0   0   4   0   0   0 3C 80 40   0 _____<_@_
    408024   8A 49 40   0   2 81 40   0 90 80 40   0 B3 80 40   0 _I@__@_@_3_@_
    408034   90 80 40   0   0   0   0   0 44 55 4D 50 45 54 20 43 __@_____DUMPET C
    408044   52 20 2E 22 20 48 45 4C 4C 4F 2C 20 57 4F 52 4C R ." HELLO, WORL
    408054   44 21 22 20 3B   0   0   0   0   0   0   0   0   0   0   0 D!" ;_____
    408064    0   0   0   0   0   0   0   0   0   0   0   0   0   0   0   0 _____
    408074    0   0   0   0   0   0   0   0   0   0   0   0   0   0   0   0 _____
 0  0  0  >
```

Here you will see the values of all system variable, and many
familiar characters you had typed. Starting at memory location
40803C is the Terminal Input Buffer (TIB) which stores the
command lines you typed, to be interpreted by the Forth text
interpreter.

Test Programs

When I implemented a eForth system, I always tested it by
compiling and executing the following new words:

```
: TEST1 1 2 3 4 ;
: TEST2 IF 1 ELSE 2 THEN . ;
: TEST3 10 FOR R@ . NEXT ;
: TEST4 10 BEGIN DUP WHILE DUP . 1- REPEAT ;
```

If everything goes well, the console window will look like this:

```
■ C:\Irvine\Project32_VS2015\Debug\Project.exe                          – □ X
0 0 0 0 >
0 0 0 0 > sp0
0 0 0 408004 > DUMP
  408004   7C FF 18   0 7C F7 18   0 10  0  0  0  4  0  0  0 !___!u_____
  408014    4  0  0  0  0  0  0  0  4  0  0  0 3C 80 40  0 _____< _@_
  408024   8A 49 40  0  2 81 40  0 90 80 40  0 B3 80 40  0 _I@___@___@_3_@_
  408034   90 80 40  0  0  0  0  0  0 44 55 4D 50 45 54 20 43 __@_____DUMPET C
  408044   52 20 2E 22 20 48 45 4C 4C 4F 2C 20 57 4F 52 4C R ." HELLO, WORL
  408054   44 21 22 20 3B  0  0  0  0  0  0  0  0  0  0  0 D!" ;_____
  408064    0  0  0  0  0  0  0  0  0  0  0  0  0  0  0  0 _____
  408074    0  0  0  0  0  0  0  0  0  0  0  0  0  0  0  0 _____
0 0 0 0 >
0 0 0 0 >
0 0 0 0 > : TEST1 1 2 3 4 ;
0 0 0 0 > TEST1
1 2 3 4 > : TEST2 IF 1 ELSE 2 THEN . ;
1 2 3 4 > 0 TEST2 2
1 2 3 4 > 1 TEST2 1
1 2 3 4 > : TEST3 10 FOR R@ . NEXT ;
1 2 3 4 > TEST3 10 F E D C B A 9 8 7 6 5 4 3 2 1 0
1 2 3 4 > : TEST4 10 BEGIN DUP WHILE DUP . 1- REPEAT DROP ;
1 2 3 4 > TEST4 10 F E D C B A 9 8 7 6 5 4 3 2 1
1 2 3 4 >
1 2 3 4 >
1 2 3 4 >
```

Decompiler

Another interesting tool command is SEE. It decompiles a colon word. Here we had compiled these words: TEST, TEST1, TEST2, TEST3 and TEST4. Type:

```
SEE TEST
```

and then hit the Enter key twice really fast, and you will see the results of decompiler:

```
C:\Irvine\Project32_VS2015\Debug\Project.exe
1 2  3  4 > TEST4 10 F E D C B A 9 8 7 6 5 4 3 2 1
1 2  3  4 >
1 2  3  4 >
1 2  3  4 > SEE TEST
43 40 0 ."! D 48 45 4C 4C 4F 2C 20 57 4F 52 4C 44 21 EXIT 90 80 40 0 5 54 45 53
54 31 41 35 40 0 dolit 1 0 0 0 dolit 2 0 0 0 dolit 3 0 0 0 dolit 4 0 0 0 EXIT B
7 80 40 0 5 54 45 53 54 32 41 35 40 0 ?branch B 81 40 0 dolit 1 0 0 0 branch 13
81 40 0 dolit 2 0 0 0 . EXIT E9 80 40 0 5 54 45 53 54 33 41 35 40 0 dolit 10 0 0
0 >R R@ . donxt 35 81 40 0 EXIT 1F 81 40 0 5 54 45 53 54 34 41 35 40 0 dolit 10
0 0 0 DUP ?branch 7F 81 40 0 DUP . 1- branch 5F 81 40 0 DROP EXIT 1 3B 0 0 4 54
45 53 54 34 0 0 0 0 0 0 31 34 0 0 0 0 0 0 0 0 0 0 0 0 0 0 0 0 0 0 0 0 0 0 0 0 0
0 0 0 0 0 0 0 0 0 0 0 0 0 0 0 0 0 0 0 0 0 0 0 0 0 0 0 0 0 0 0 0 0 0 0 0 33 33 0 0
0 0 0 0 0 0 0 0 0 0 0 0 0 0 0 0 0 0 0 0 0 0 0 0 0 0 0 0 0 0 0 0 0 0 0 0 0 0 0 0 0
0 0 0 0 0 0 0 0 0 0 0 0 0 0 0 0 0 0 0 0 0 0 0 0 0 0 0 0 0 0 0 0 0 0 0 0 0 0 0 0 0
0 0 0 0 0 0 0 0 0 0 0 0 0 0 0 0 0 0 0 0 0 0 0 0 0 0 0 0 0 0 0 0 0 0 0 0 0 0 0 0 0
0 0 0 0 0 0 0 0 0 0 0 0 0 0 0 0 0 0 0 0 0 0 0 0 0 0 0 0 0 0 0 0 0 0 0 0 0 0 0 0 0
0 0 0 0 0 0 0 0 0 0 0 0 0 0 0 0 0 0 0 0 0 0 0 0 0 0 0 0 0 0 0 0 0 0 0 0 0 0 0 0 0
0 0 0 0 0 0 0 0 0 0 0 0 0 0 0 0 0 0 0 0 0 0 0 0 0 0 0 0 0 0 0 0 0 0 0 0 0 0 0 0 0
0 0 0 0 0 0 0 0 0 0 0 0 0 0 0 0 0 0 0 0 0 0 0 0 0 0 0 0 0 0 0 0 0 0 0 0 0 0 0 0 0
0 0 0 0 0 0 0 0 0 0 0 0 0 0 0 0 0 0 0 0 0 0 0 0 0 0 0 0 0 0 0 0 0 0 0 0 0 0 0 0 0
0 0 0 0 0 0 0 0 0 0 0 0 0 0 0 0 0 0 0 0 0 0 0 0 0 0 0 0 0 0 0 0 0 0 0 0 0 0 0 0 0
0 0 0 0 0 0 0 0 0 0 0 0 0 0 0 0 0 0 0 0 0 0 0 0 0 0 0 0 0 0 0 0 0 0 0 0 0 0 0 0 0
0 0 0 0 0 0 0 0 0 0 0 0 0 0 0 0 0 0 0 0 0 0 0 0 0 0 0 0 0 0 0 0 0 0 0 0 0 0 0 0 0
0 0 0 0 0 0 0 0 0 0 0 0 0 0 0 0 0 0 0 0 0 0 0 0 0 0 0 0 0 0 0 0 0 0 0 0 0 0 0 0 0
0 0 0 0 0 0 0 0 0 0 0 0 0 0 0 0 0 0 0 0 0 0 0 0 0 0 0 0 0 0 0 0 0 0 0 0 0 0 0 0 0
```

My finger was not fast enough, and the decompiler ran over a large chunk of empty memory. On the top of display, you can see the contents of TEST-TEST4. The decompiler does not try to recover the source code completely. It tries to show you the Forth words compiled in the memory. Data other than code field addresses are displayed in bytes, and they include link field addresses, branch addresses, literal values, names of words, and compiled string literals. They will make sense when you get to know Forth well.

In the next picture, I show you the memory dump starting at the code field address of TEST. It is another view of compiled colon words. In 128 bytes, you will see only the contents of TEST, TEST1 and TEST2.

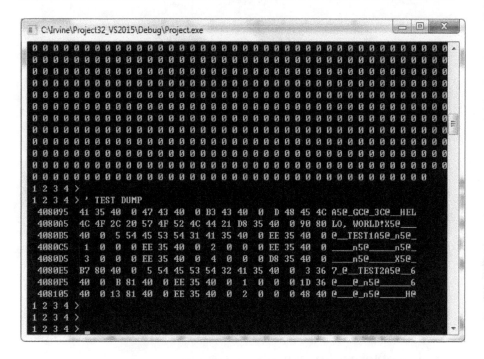

OK. Here I've shown you how 86eForth v5.2 was assembled and activated under Visual Studio. A few interactive exercises served to show you how you could use it and extend it. The purpose of this eForth system is not to write big applications in Windows, because then I have to dive into the very complicated Windows environment. The purpose is to show you a minimal command set that constitutes an interactive Virtual Forth Engine. This model can be easily ported to any computer with reasonable resources. It is best used in embedded microcontrollers for instrumental and robotic applications. It serves to remind you that the 'e' in eForth stands for 'easy' and 'embedded'.

Chapter 5. - eForth Virtual Forth Engine

Before diving directly into eForth, I would like to discuss the general principles of a Virtual Forth Engine and many other system design issues so that you have a better overall view of the eForth system when investigating the detailed structures and code in eForth.

I think the following topics are the most important in understanding Forth:

- Inner (address) interpreter

- Outer (text) interpreter

- Dual stack architecture

- List of tokens (execution addresses)

- Linked dictionary

- Memory space

Using a real eForth implementation helps to make these topics clear. It is also interesting to note that these topics appear quite naturally in the beginning of the eForth MASM source listing as we set up MASM before starting assembling any code.

In effect, it allows us to read the source code from the beginning to the end in its natural sequence. I had some reservation in that we might not be able to present the eForth system clearly without going back and forth over the source listing, because the logic of the system might not follow the loading order. In the end, it worked out perfectly.

Inner and Outer Interpreters

Like Prajna and Samadhi in Zen, the most important concepts in Forth can be summarized in two components, the inner interpreter and the outer interpreter. The inner interpreter runs the computer hardware to execute Forth commands or words. The outer interpreter, or the text interpreter, is the operating system. It accepts a list of Forth commands from you in text form and executes these commands in sequence. It employs a very simple syntax rule:

Commands are separated by spaces.

Text interpreter processes a list of Forth commands or words, separated by spaces or white characters like tabs, line feeds, and carriage returns:

```
<list of commands>
```

The text interpreter reads a line of text, parses out commands, and execute them in sequence. Commands are separated by spaces, like words in English. It can easily pick up commands one after the other and executes them in sequence.

Because of this very simple syntax rule, the outer interpreter is very simple yet very powerful. Forth is made even more powerful by allowing you to compile new Forth commands, which replaces lists of existing commands. The syntax of compiling new commands is:

```
:   <name>   <list of commands>   ;
```

':' is a Forth command, which changes the text interpreter to a compiler. The compiler takes the following <name>, which is a character string, for the name of a new command. The compiler compiles the following <list of commands> into a token list, stored in memory. The command ';' terminates <list of commands>. New commands built by ':' are generally called high level Forth words, or colon words.

When text interpreter encounters the new command <name>, it calls an inner interpreter to execute the compiled token list. This inner interpreter is also called an address interpreter, because the tokens are actually code field addresses of Forth commands.

A new command replaces a list of existing commands; thereby elevates Forth language to a higher level of abstraction. Number of new commands is not limited. Levels of abstraction are also not limited. Compiling lists into commands is generally the most efficient way to solved programming problems. In this aspect, Forth is very similar to LISP.

There are many other types of Forth words besides colon words. In 86eForth v5.2, we have code words which contain native machine instructions, constants, variables, and arrays. Each of these different types of Forth words are executed differently by their respective inner interpreters. An inner interpreter in Forth is generally a very short code fragment pointed to by the address in the code field of every command in memory. Each type of Forth commands employs a unique inner interpreter to provide special run time behavior to this type of commands.

Virtual Forth Engine

Forth is a computer model which can be implemented on any real CPU with reasonable resources. This model is often called a Virtual Forth Engine. The minimal components of a Virtual Forth Engine are:

- A dictionary in memory to hold all execution commands called words.

- A return stack to hold return addresses of commands yet to be executed.

- A data stack to hold parameters passing among commands.

- A variable area in RAM memory holding all the system variables.

- A word set which moves and often changes data in memory and on stacks.

- The word set can be extended at run time.

The eForth Model is a detailed specification of a universal Virtual Forth Engine which had been implemented on many microprocessors and microcontrollers, so that they behaved identically in executing an identical command set. This first implementation of eForth used Intel 8086 CPU as a guide to implementations on other CPU's. Here we will try to describe precisely the behavior of the generic eForth Model. I use thed 8086 instruction set in the first edition of this book to describe the exact behavior of this Virtual Forth Engine.

The original eForth Model, 86eForth v1.0 released in 1990, assumed a 16-bit 8086 CPU. As the 80x86 CPUs evolved into 32 and even 64 bit, it is necessary to modify this model to suit the later, more advanced CPUs. In this new implementation, 86eForth v5.2, I use a 32-bit 586 class CPU as a host. The eForth command set is significantly reduced. Many high level Forth commands are now coded in machine instructions to optimize its performance.

The following 32-bit registers are used in this Virtual Forth Engine:

Forth Register	CPU Register	Function
IP	ESI	Interpreter Pointer
SP	ESP	Data Stack Pointer
RP	EBP	Return Stack Pointer
WP	EAX	Word or Work Pointer

Inner Interpreters

In memory, each command or word has a record containing 4 fields: a link field pointing to the name field of its prior command, a name field containing the ASCII characters for the name of this command, a code field pointing to executable machine code (inner interpreter) for this command, and a parameter field containing data required by this command. There are two principal types of commands used in eForth: low level code words whose parameter field contains machine instructions, and high level colon words whose parameter field contains a list of tokens. Token can take many different forms, depending upon implementation. In this model, a token is the code field address of a command in memory. Tokens are 4 bytes in length. The length of a parameter field varies depending upon the complexity of the word.

In the code field of a low level code word, there is an address pointing to the parameter field 4 bytes after the code field. In the parameter field there is a list of machine instructions of the native 80x86 CPU. The machine instructions are terminated by two instructions, generally assembled by a macro named $NEXT. The function of $NEXT is to fetch the token pointed to by the Interpreter Pointer IP (ESI), increment IP to point to the next token in a token list, and execute the token just fetched. Since a token points to a code field containing the address of executable machine instructions, executing a token means jumping indirectly to the parameter field pointed to by the token. $NEXT thus allows the Virtual Forth Engine to execute a list of tokens with very little CPU overhead. In 86eForth v5.2, $NEXT is a macro two machine instructions as shown below.

```
$NEXT    MACRO
         LODSD                          read the next code
                                        address into AX
         JMP      DWORD PTR [EAX]       jump indirectly to the
                                        code address
         ENDM
```

In other CPUs, especially the less capable 8 bit processors, $NEXT could assemble a JMP <NEXT> instruction. <NEXT> is then a centralized routine which causes the next token to be fetched and executed while IP is incremented to point to the next token.

This scheme of jumping indirectly to an execution routine pointed to by a token is commonly referred to as 'Indirect Threaded Model'. Since the very beginning, Chuck Moore used this model in most of his Forth implementations. The other scheme 'Direct Thread Model' used in many newer Forth systems put executable machine instructions in a variable length code field. The executable code defines the behavior of the command. A third scheme uses the pointer to point to a token table where addresses of executable code are stored. This is called 'Token Threaded Model'. Direct Threaded Model was chosen in the original 86eForth v1.0 because it was conceptually simpler and faster in execution. In the current implementation, indirect threading is required, because new commands cannot be added to the .code segment, and machine instructions cannot be executed in the .data segment. Here, a high level colon word contain only address pointers, and can be compiled and executed in the .data segment.

In a code word, a 4 byte address in its code field points to the following parameter field which contains a machine instruction routine, performing the function of this command. This machine instruction routine must be terminated by two instructions assembled by $NEXT, which continues executing the next token in a token list calling this command.

In a colon word, a 4 byte address in the code field points to a machine instruction routine which processes the token list in the parameter field following the code field. This token list processing routine is named DOLST. DOLST pushes the contents in IP (ESI) onto the return stack, copies the address of the first token in its code field into IP and then calls $NEXT. $NEXT will then execute the list of tokens in the parameter field.

```
DOLST:                                colon word interpreter
        XCHG    EBP,ESP               exchange the return and
                                      data stack pointers
        PUSH    ESI                   push on return stack
        XCHG    EBP,ESP               restore the pointers
        ADD     EAX,CELLL             Point to parameter field
        MOV     ESI,EAX               new list address
        LODSD                         read the next code address
                                      into AX
        JMP     DWORD PTR             jump indirectly to the code
                [EAX]                 address
```

The last token in the token list of a colon word must be EXIT. EXIT is a code word which undoes what DOLST accomplished. EXIT pops the top item on the return stack into the IP (ESI) register. Consequently, IP points to the token following the colon word just executed. EXIT then invokes $NEXT which continues processing of the token list, briefly interrupted by the last colon word in this token list.

```
$CODE    4,'EXIT',EXITT      EXIT ( -- ) Terminate a colon
                             definition.
XCHG     EBP,ESP             exchange pointers
POP      ESI                 pop return stack
XCHG     EBP,ESP             restore stack pointers
$NEXT
```

$NEXTis the inner interpreter of code words, and DOLST is the inner interpreter of high level colon words and are often referred to as an address interpreter. They are the foundations of a Virtual Forth Engine.

Based on the above mechanism to execute code words and colon words, a Virtual Forth Engine can be constructed using a small set of machine dependent code words and a much larger set of machine independent colon words, giving it the capability of executing commands you type on a keyboard, and compiling more words to extend the basic Forth system. The word QUIT at the highest level will interact with you through a terminal. It is called the 'Text Interpreter', or the 'Outer Interpreter'. The Forth text interpreter has two modes of operating. In the interpreting mode, it accepts a list of words and executes them in sequence. In the compiling mode, it builds new colon words by compiling lists of words into lists of tokens in memory. It is equivalent to a conventional operating system with an integral command interpreter and a compiler for adding new commands.

To learn Forth, it is important to keep in mind constantly the functions of the inner/address interpreter and of the outer/text interpreter. They are the crucial elements which make a Virtual Forth Engine tick.

The text interpreter /compiler has the capability of compiling new words into memory. A new word contains a list of existing words, like a sequence of subroutines. You can thus expand the scope and capability of an elementary Forth system by adding more words. By adding more words based upon previously defined words, a Forth system can easily grow and encompasses solutions to a wide range of applications.

eForth Words

There are 110 high level colon words in eForth, built on 71 low level code words, in this 86eForth v5.2 system. The high level word set is required to build the outer interpreter and the associated utility words. As the outer interpreter itself represents a fairly substantial application, the word set necessary to build the outer interpreter forms a very solid foundation to build most other applications. However, for any real world application one would not expect that this eForth word set is sufficient. The beauty of Forth is that in programming an application, you design and implement a new word set best tailored to your application. Forth is an open system. It assumes that no operating system can be complete and all-encompassing. You understand best your needs, and you know the best way to accomplish you goal.

Another way of looking at the eForth word set is to divide it into the commonly used words and the system words which are needed to build the outer interpreter, but are rarely used in applications. Among the 181 words in eForth, 134 words can be classified as commonly useful words and 87 words are system words. In this implementation, commonly used words are defined in upper case and system words are defined in lower case. As this system is case sensitive, and programs are assumed to be written mostly in upper case, you have to make a special effort to access system words.

The set of 134 common Forth words contains the Forth words which are universally supported in most Forth systems. They include data stack and return stack words, memory accessing words, math and logical words, control structure words, defining words, and some utility words. To use Forth fluently, you have to fully understand these words and use them efficiently to compose new words which will solve your applications.

The set of 87 system words are defined to support the construction of outer interpreter in eForth. They are necessary in building a Forth system and are not needed for day-to-day programming. If you are building applications on an eForth system, only in rare occasions you will have to use words in this set. If you have to build an eForth system or port it to a special CPU, you must understand this word set very well because they are tools you must have to build or change eForth system.

Following table shows the eForth word set

System and I/O Words	`BYE ?KEY KEY EMIT`
Kernel Words	`dolit dolst EXIT EXECUTE next ?branch branch ! @ C! C@ rp@ rp! R> R@ >R sp@ sp! DROP DUP SWAP OVER 0< AND OR XOR UM+`
System Variables	`sp0 rp0 base tmp span >in #tib 'eval 'number hld context cp last`
Common Functions	`?DUP ROT 2DROP 2DUP + NOT NEGATE DNEGATE -ABS = U< < MAX MIN WITHIN`
Divide and Multiply	`UM/MOD M/MOD /MOD MOD / UM* * M* */MOD */`
Miscellaneous	`1+ 1- 2+ 2- 2* 2/ 4+ 4- 4* BL >char depth PICK`
Memory Access	`+! 2! 2@ COUNT HERE PAD TIB @EXECUTE CMOVE FILL pack$`
Numeric Output	`digit extract <# HOLD # #S SIGN #> str HEX DECIMAL`
Numeric Input	`digit? number?`
Basic I/O	`NUF? SPACE TYPE CR do$ $"| ."| .R U.R U. . ?`
Parsing	`(parse) parse .( ( \ CHAR token WORD`
Dictionary Search	`name> same? find name?`
Terminal Response	`^h tap ktap accept expect quary`
Error Handling	`ABORT abort"| ABORT"`
Text Interpreter	`$interpret [ .ok ?stack eval`
Shell	`preset QUIT`

Compiler	`' ALLOT , [compile] compile literal $."`
Structures	`FOR BEGIN NEXT UNTIL AGAIN IF AHEAD REPEAT THEN AFT ELSE WHILE ABORT" $" ."`
Name Compiler	`?unique $,n`
Forth Compiler	`$compile overt ; ] : IMMEDIATE`
Defining Words	`CREATE CONSTANT VARIABLE`
Tools	`DUMP .S >NAME .ID SEE WORDS`
Hardware Reset	`COLD`

Memory Space

The most important contribution by von Neumann to the computer design was the recognition that a single, uniform memory device can be used to store program and data, contrasting to the then prevailing architectures in which program and data were stored separately and most often using very different storage media. It greatly simplified the design of computers and had become the dominant computer architecture for all the important computer families ever since.

Memory space is a concept of paramount importance in computer hardware and assembly programming, but often hidden and protected in most conventional high level languages. High level languages and operating systems hide the addressable memory space from you in order to protect the operating system, because there are very sensitive areas in the memory space and unintentional alterations to the information stored in these areas would cause the system to malfunction or even to crash. The point of view from the operating system and from the computer priesthood, is that these sensitive areas must be protected at all cost, and they are the reserved territory of the systems programmers. Ordinary applications programmers are allocated only enough space to run their programs safely, for their own good.

Forth opens the entire memory space to you. You can freely store data and code into memory and retrieve them from the memory. Coming with the freedom is the responsibility of handling the memory correctly.

All prior eForth systems assumed that the memory space is open for reading, writing, and executing. However, when I tried to implement eForth under Visual Studio, I learned that new MASM assembler bundled with C++ observes very strong memory segmentation rules, and does not allow applications to write into the .code segment. It also does not allow applications to execute code stored in .data segment. It basically returns to the computer medieval age. In order to impose a Virtual Forth Engine against these obstacles, I had to change this eForth system to the indirect thread model. All predefined Forth words are assembled in the .code segment. System variables and string buffers are allocated in .data segment. In addition, new colon words are compiled into a big buffer in the .data segment.

By the way, SmallWin.inc supplied by Kip Irvine allocated a 4096 byte segment for .stack. This eForth uses the .stack segment thus allocated to store both the data stack and the return stack.

Allocation of memory segments are as the following:

Segment	Length	Function
.stack	4096 bytes	Data stack and return stack
.code	8192 bytes	Dictionary of assembled Forth words
.data	60 bytes	System variables
	80 bytes	Terminal input buffer
	16K bytes	Dictionary for new colon words

Data Segment

In the good old days of 8-bit microprocessors, we were very happy to have 64K bytes of memory where we could place ROM and RAM memories any way we saw fit. Then, Intel invented the segmented memory architecture to allow memory beyond 64K. It designated code segment, stack segment, and several data segments, but did not restrict read/write/execute behavior in software. In the early eForth implementations, I collapsed the segments together and used it freely. Forth is extensible, and I could add new code and new data to RAM memory freely.

With the new MASM under C++, Visual Studio imposes very strict rules in the use of memory segments, assuming that self-modifying code is illegal and enemy number 1 to the programming public. Therefore, you cannot change your code in the .code segment at run time. You can only change data you stored in the .data segment, and you cannot execute code stored in the .data segment. In this new 86eForth v5.2, I circumvented these restrictions with indirect thread model. Here, all code words are assembled in the .code segment, with all colon words required by the Virtual Forth Engine to function. However, new colon words added by you will be stored in the .data segment. These new colon words can be executed by Virtual Forth Engine, because colon words contain only data and addresses, and there is no machine instruction whatsoever. As far as the host CPU is concerned, they are simply data and do not alert the CPU protective mechanism.

I have reduced the system variables in 86eForth v5.2 to the minimum, 13 in total. They are absolutely necessary for the text interpreter and the compiler to function properly. In addition, there is a terminal input buffer to store input characters from a keyboard and a big dictionary buffer to store new colon words. The empty space above the added colon words is used as floating buffers for various purposes.

```
.data
UZERO      DD 0              start of variable area
_SPP       DD 0              bottom of the data stack
_RPP       DD 0              bottom of the return stack
_BASE      DD BASEE          radix base for numeric I/O
_TMP       DD 0              temporary storage
_IN        DD 0              current character pointer to input string
_SPAN      DD 0              character count received by EXPECT
_NTIB      DD 0              end of input string
_TIBB      DD _TIB           beginning of input string
_EVAL      DD 0              execution vector for EVAL
_HLD       DD 0              next character in numeric output string
_CNTXT     DD OFFSET         name field of last word in dictionary
           LASTN
_CP        DD _CPP           top of dictionary
```

```
_LASTN      DD OFFSET      initial CONTEXT
            LASTN
ULAST       DD 0           end of variable area
_TIB        DD 20          terminal input buffer
            DUP(0)
_CPP        DD 4096        user dictionary
            DUP(0)
```

Word Records

Predefined Forth words, both low level and high level, are assembled into a linearly linked dictionary in .code segment. New high level Forth words are compiled into a big buffer in .data segment. Low level words cannot be assembled into .data segment, because they cannot be executed.

Each word is a record with 4 fields:

Field	Length	Function
Link	4 bytes	name field of previous word
Name	Variable	name of word and lexicon byte
Code	4 byte	pointer to executable code
Parameter	Variable	instructions, tokens, data

Following figure shows the record structure:

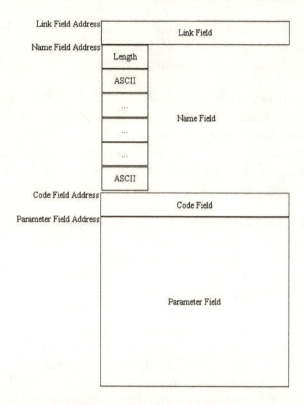

The addresses of the first bytes in these fields are called, respectively, link field address (lfa), name field address (nfa), code field address (cfa), and parameter field address (pfa). Abbreviations of these field addresses will be used throughout this book.

The dictionary is a linked list of all word records. The link field contains a pointer pointing to the name field of the prior word. The link list starts at the last word COLD assembled in the dictionary. Word searching also starts here. The first word BYE, which terminates the list and searching, has a zero in its link field, indicating the end of list.

86eForth v5.2 uses the 'Indirect Thread Model'. Each word has a code field in the dictionary. The code field address is considered the token of this word. The code field contains a pointer to executable code. In a low level machine code word, the code field contains a pointer pointing to the parameter field, which is 4 byte after the code field. Executable code are stored in the parameter field, terminated by the inner interpreter $NEXT. $NEXT is defined as an in-line expanded macro (LODWD JMP [EAX]) which fetches the next token from a token list and executes that token.

In a low level code word, the address in code field is the parameter field address, 4 bytes after the code field. The parameter field contains a machine instruction routine, to be executed by underlying CPU. The machine instruction routine is generally terminated by a $NEXT macro, which assembles two instructions LODSD JMP [EAX], the inner interpreter of eForth.

In a high level colon word, the code field points to a DOLST machine instruction routine, which process the contents of the parameter field as a token list. The token list is generally terminated by a code word EXIT, which is the address interpreter of eForth, together with DOLST.

Other types of words like constants, variables, and arrays have their own interpreters. The code field in a constant word points to a routine DOCON. The code fields of variables and array words point to another routine DOVAR. The size of parameter fields in constants and variables is 4 bytes, containing the value of a constant or variable. The size of parameter field in an array word is variable, allocated when the array is constructed. In 86eForth v5.2 the code fields and parameter fields of these words are shown as the following figure:

Code Word

$+4	Machine Instructions	LODWD	JMP [EAX]

Colon Word

DOLST	Token List	EXIT

Constant

DOCON	n

Variable

DOVAR	n

Create Array

DOVAR	Array

In the dictionary, words are linked through the link fields. The address in a link field is the name field address of the previous word. This threading scheme optimizes the dictionary search. With the link field address on the data stack, commands @ @ will yield the length byte and the first 3 character in the name field of the previous word. The lowest 16 bit value is compared to the length and first byte of the name to be searched for, and a quick decision can be made to look for the next word, or to compare the rest of the name. The rest of the name must be compared byte-by-byte, because the name fields are of variable length, and are not aligned to 32-bit word boundaries.

Assembly Macros

Several macros are defined in the MASM assembly source code to simplify assembling of the Forth dictionary. The macro $CODE assembles the header of a low level code word, including the link field, the name field, and the code field. A label is also created marking the code field address, which are later referred to as tokens. The first byte in the name field is special, and is referred to as a lexicon byte. The lower 5 bits in lexicon byte store the character length of the name, Bit 6 stores a compile-only bit, indicating that this words can be used only in the compiler. Bit 7 stores an immediate bit, indicating that this command must be executed immediately during compiling.

$CODE assembles the parameter field address in the code field. Therefore, when a code word is executed, the Virtual Forth Engine hands the machine instruction routine in the parameter field to the host CPU for execution. An extra machine cycle seems to be wasted in this indirect thread model. The advantage is that all the other types of high level words have a uniform mechanism to process a variety of data in the parameter field.

_LINK retains the name field address of this word to build the link field of the next word. All words in the dictionary are thus linearly linked list, which can be searched to find a word by its name. _CODE retains the code field address and helps assembling the parameter field address into the code field.

```
_LINK    = 0                      Save link field address
_CODE    = 0                      Save code field address
$CODE    MACRO LEX,NAME,LABEL     Macro for code words
         DD _LINK                 Build a link field
         _LINK = $                Save name field address for
                                  next link
         DB LEX,NAME              Lexicon byte and name string
LABEL:   CODE = $                 Save code field address
         DD _CODE+CELLL           Store pfa in code field
         ENDM
```

The second macro $COLON assembles the header of a high level colon word. It assembles a link field and a name field, just like $CODE. However, it assembles the address of DOLST in the code field. When a colon words is executed, DOLST pushes the current IP on the return stack and copies the parameter field address of this colon word into IP register. At the end of DOLST, $NEXT is executed and the token list in the parameter field is processed.

```
$COLON     MACRO LEX,NAME,LABEL    Macro for colon words
           DD _LINK                Build link field
           _LINK = $               Save name field address for
                                   next link
           DB LEX,NAME             Lexicon byte and name string
LABEL:     DD DOLST                Address interpreter for colon
                                   word
           ENDM
```

Finally, the macro $NEXT is defined to assemble the inner
interpreter at the end of every code word. For a 32-bit 80x86 CPU,
the inner interpreter consists of two machine instructions: LODSD
and JMP [EAX]. It loads an address pointed to by IP (ESI) register
into EAX register, while increment IP by 4, and then jump to the
address pointed to by EAX. 80x86 is therefore a very efficient host
CPU for a Virtual Forth Machine. Only two machine instructions are
necessary to implement the inner interpreter for code words. The
implementation of address interpreter DOLST will be discussed
shortly.

```
$NEXT      MACRO                   Macro to add inner
                                   interpreter to end code words
           LODSD                   Read the next code address
                                   into EAX
           JMP DWORD PTR [EAX]     Jump indirectly to the code
                                   address in EAX
           ENDM
```

MAIN

Windows starts executing the machine routine MAIN at the
beginning of .code segment. What we have to do here is to set up the
80x86 CPU so that it will emulate a Virtual Forth. All pertinent
registers have to be initialized properly. MASM allocates a .stack
segment for a stack handling calling and returns of subroutines. The
top of stack when entering eForth is stored in ESP register. It is used
by the Virtual Forth Engine as its data stack. Four 0's are pushed on
the stack buffering Forth data stack and the Windows system stack.
The return stack required by Forth is initialized 2K bytes above the

data stack, and the return stack pointer in EBP register is initialized accordingly.

Now we are ready to start the Forth engine. Simply jumping indirectly to COLD will do it. COLD is coded as a colon word, containing a list of tokens. COLD sends out a sign-on message and then executes ABORT, which calls QUIT, the text interpreter, which contains an infinite loop to receive commands from you and executes them repeatedly.

```
.code                           Start of code segment
MAIN    PROC                    Entrance
        XOR     EAX,EAX
        PUSH    EAX             Init data stack
        PUSH    EAX             Clear top of data stack
        PUSH    EAX
        PUSH    EAX
        MOV     EAX,ESP         Initialize data stack pointer ESP
        MOV     _SPP,EAX        Save ESP for ABORT
        SUB     EAX,800H
        MOV     EBP,EAX         Initialize return stack pointer EBP
        MOV     _RPP,EAX        Save EBP for QUIT
        CLD                     Clear direction flag, incrementing ESI
        MOV     EAX,COLD        High level cold start
        JMP     DWORD PTR       Jump indirectly to the code address
                [EAX]
```

Address Interpreter

The words DOLST and EXIT encapsulate a token list in a colon word, which begins with a pointer to DOLST, followed by a list of tokens, and terminated by pointer to EXIT. DOLST pushes the current Instruction Pointer IP, which is in the ESI register, on the return stack and then pops the pointer to the first token into IP from the data stack. When $NEXT is executed, the tokens in the list are executed consecutively.

DOLST is therefore the address interpreter of high level colon words. It is the crucial mechanism which executes a high level token in a token list and then returns control to the calling token list.

```
DOLST:                              Colon word address interpreter
        XCHG    EBP,ESP             Exchange return and data stack
                                    pointers
        PUSH    ESI                 Push IP on return stack
        XCHG    EBP,ESP             Restore stack pointers
        ADD     EAX,CELLL           EAX now points to parameter
                                    field
        MOV     ESI,EAX             New list address in IP
        LODSD                       Read the next code address into
                                    EAX
        JMP     DWORD PTR           Jump indirectly to the code field
                [EAX]               address
```

EXIT is at the end of all token lists. EXIT pops the execution address saved on the return stack back into the IP register and thus restores the condition before the token was entered. Execution of the calling token list will continue.

```
$CODE   4,'EXIT',EXITT             EXIT ( -- ) Terminate a colon
                                    definition.
XCHG    EBP,ESP                     Exchange stack pointers
POP     ESI                         Pop return stack to IP
XCHG    EBP,ESP                     Restore stack pointers
$NEXT
```

CONSTANT and VARIABLE are important commands for you to store and retrieve often used numeric data. The difference between them is that a constant returns a value, and a variable returns an address pointing to a value. They are records similar to a colon word. They have parameter fields of 4 byte size, and their code fields contain pointers pointing to DOCON and DOVAR routines, respectively.

When DOCON or DOVAR is executed, EAX points to the code field. DOVAR pushes the address of its parameter field, EAX+4, on the data stack and returns. DOCON pushes the contents of its parameter field [EAX+4] on the data stack and returns. DOCON th thus the constant interpreter, and DOVAR is the variable interpreter. They are very similar to the address interpreter DOLST, though they handle only one cell of data in a parameter field.

```
DOVAR:                              Variable interpreter
        ADD     EAX,CELLL           Increment EAX pointing to
                                    parameter field
        PUSH    EAX                 Push pfa on data stack
        $NEXT


DOCON:                              Constant interpreter
        ADD     EAX,CELLL           Increment EAX pointing to
                                    parameter field
        PUSH    DWORD PTR           Push value in parameter field
                [EAX]               on data stack
        $NEXT
```

Chapter 6. - eForth Kernel

For the very beginning, we wanted to develop a complete Forth system with a kernel, which is a minimal set of primitives or code commands. In Forth community, this has been an active controversy since day one. What had been selected as the eForth code word set were all the operations we cannot synthesize conveniently and effectively with high level colon words. Actually, eForth provided a good platform to test the effectiveness of this set of primitive code words. We had observed that in certain small 8-bit controller like 8051, this code word set really slows down the processor. However, the same code word set proved to be quite adequate in the 16-bit processors like 8086 and 68000. In the 32-bit implementation for 80386 in the protected mode, eForth is blazingly fast.

Since most microprocessors have fairly good machine instructions, it is quite easy to rewrite the eForth kernel for any target microprocessor. The assembly code in the eForth Model serves to clarify any discrepancy in the functional specifications of the code words.

One of the most important features of eForth is the small machine dependent kernel, which allows it to be ported to other CPU's very conveniently. The selection of words in this kernel is based on the criteria that they are very difficult if not impossible to synthesize from other Forth words. From this set of code words, all other words can be synthesized. The kernel words can be classified as following:

System interface	BYE, ?KEY, KEY, EMIT
Inner interpreters	DOLIT, DOLST, DONXT, ?BRANCH, BRANCH, EXECUTE, EXIT
Memory access	! , @, C!, C@
Return stack	RP@, RP!, R>, R@, R>
Data stack	SP@, SP!, DROP, DUP, SWAP, OVER
Logic	0<, AND, OR, XOR
Arithmetic	UM+

System Interface

BYE returns control from eForth back to the operating system.
?KEY and KEY accept input from a keyboard, and EMIT sends a
character to the console display. eForth communicates with you
through these words which supports terminal interactions and file
download/upload.

```
$CODE      3,'BYE',BYE       BYE ( -- ) Exit eForth.
Invoke     ExitProcess,0     Return to Windows
```

?KEY inspects the terminal device and returns a character and a true
flag if the character has been received and is waiting to be retrieved.
If no character was received, ?KEY simply returns a false flag.

```
        $CODE   4,'?KEY',QKEY     ?RX ( -- c T | F ) Return input
                                  character and true, or a false if
                                  no input.
        XOR     EBX,EBX           EBX=0 setup for false flag
        XOR     EAX,EAX           EAX=0 prepare to receive one
                                  character
        call    ReadKey           Call system service
        JZ      SHORT QRX3        Got a key? Jump if not.
        PUSH    EAX               Save character
        DEC     EBX               Make a true flag
QRX3:   PUSH    EBX               Save flag
        $NEXT
```

KEY, on the other hand, waits until a character is received from the
terminal device and returns its ASCII code.

```
$CODE      3,'KEY',KEY       KEY ( -- c ) Wait for and return an input
                             character.
call       ReadChar          Wait for character
AND        EAX,07FH          Mask non-printable
PUSH       EAX               Save character
$NEXT
```

EMIT sends a character on the data stack to the terminal device. BYE, ?KEY, KEY and EMIT are coded here as Windows system calls. In embedded applications, they will have to be coded in machine specific code to handle the specific serial I/O device.

```
$CODE   4,'EMIT',EMIT      EMIT ( c -- ) Send character c to the
                           output device.
POP     EAX
call    WriteChar          Display character on console
$NEXT
```

Kernel

EXIT is at the end of all token lists. EXIT pops the execution address saved on the return stack back into the IP register and thus restores the condition before the token was entered. Execution of the calling token list will continue.

```
$CODE   4,'EXIT',EXITT     EXIT ( -- ) Terminate a colon
                           definition.
XCHG    EBP,ESP            Exchange stack pointers
POP     ESI                Pop return stack to IP
XCHG    EBP,ESP            Restore stack pointers
$NEXT
```

EXECUTE takes a code field address from the data stack and executes that token. This powerful word allows you to execute any token which is not a part of a token list.

```
$CODE   7,'EXECUTE',EXECU  EXECUTE ( cfa -- ) Execute the
                           word at cfa.
POP     EAX                Get code field address
JMP     DWORD PTR [EAX]    Jump indirectly to the address in
                           code field
```

Integer Literals

In the token list of a colon word, it is generally assumed that tokens are execution addresses, which can be executed sequentially by the inner interpreter $NEXT. However, occasionally we do need to compile other types of data in-line with tokens. Special mechanisms must be used to tell the inner interpreter to treat these data differently. All data entries must be preceded by special tokens which can handle the data properly. A special token and its associated data form a data structure. Data structures are extensions of tokens and can be thought of as building blocks to form lists in colon words with regular tokens.

In eForth, three types of data structures are allowed: integer littorals preceded by DOLIT, address literals preceded by DONXT, ?BRANCH and BRANCH, and string literals (which will be discussed in the section of compiler). DOLIT pushes the next token onto the data stack as an integer literal. It allows numbers to be compiled as in-line literals, supplying data to the data stack at run time. eForth uses this mechanism to place constants in-line in colon words. Integer literals (DOLIT n) are compiled by LITERAL which will be discussed in the compiler section.

Integer literals are by far the most numerous data structures in colon words other than regular tokens. Address literals are used to build control structures. String literals are used to embed text strings in colon words. We will discuss address literals and string literals later.

In 80x86 eForth implementation, DOLIT is very simple and very fast. It is a preferred way to introduce integers to the data stack than constants and variables.

```
$CODE    COMPO+5,'dolit',DOLIT    DOLIT ( -- w ) Push an inline
                                  literal.
LODSD                             Load next token into EAX
PUSH     EAX                      Push it as a literal value
$NEXT
```

Address Literals

eForth uses three different types of address literals. DONXT, ?BRANCH and BRANCH are followed not by tokens but by addresses of tokens in a list to be executed next. These address literals are the building blocks upon which loop and branch structures are constructed. An address token is followed by a branch address which causes execution to be transferred to that address. The branch address most often points to a different location in the same token list.

Address literals are used to construct control structures in colon words. DONXT is compiled by NEXT. ?BRANCH is compiled by IF, WHILE and UNTIL. BRANCH is compiled by AFT, ELSE, REPEAT and AGAIN.

?BRANCH pulls the address in next token. If tos is 0, jump to this address; otherwise, ignore the address and continue executing the token following the address literal. It is a conditional jump.

```
$CODE   COMPO+7,'?branch',QBRAN   ?BRANCH ( f -- ) Branch if
                                  flag is zero.
POP     EAX                       pop flag
OR      EAX,EAX                   flag=0?
JZ      SHORT BRAN1               yes, do branch
ADD     ESI,CELLL                 point IP to next token
$NEXT
```

BRANCH pulls the address in next token, and jump to this address. It causes a unconditional jump.

```
        $CODE   COMPO+6,'branch'      BRANCH ( -- )
                ,BRAN                 Branch to an inline
                                      address.
BRAN1:  MOV     ESI,0[ESI]            IP=[IP]. Do the
                                      branching
        $NEXT
```

DONXT decrements the loop count on return stack. If the loop count become negative, pop the count off return stack, ignore the next address literal, and continue executing the next token. If count is not negative, jump to the address following DONXT.

```
      $CODE    COMPO+5,'donxt',DONXT    DONXT ( -- ) Run
                                        time code for the
                                        single index loop.
      SUB      DWORD PTR [EBP],1        decrement loop
                                        index on return
                                        stack
      JC       SHORT NEXT1             decrement below 0?
      MOV      ESI,0[ESI]             no, continue loop.
                                        IP=[IP]
      $NEXT
NEXT1: ADD     EBP,CELLL              yes, pop loop index
      ADD      ESI,CELLL              exit loop. Increment
                                        IP to next token
      $NEXT
```

It is interesting to note that eForth supplies only the down-counting FOR-NEXT definite loop structure. DO-LOOP structure and its variations in most Forth systems are not supported. The dual indexed DO-LOOP structure is much more complicated than the single index FOR-NEXT structure. Omitting DO-LOOPs simplifies eForth greatly.

At one time, Chuck Moore apologized to us that he miss-led us in adopting the DO-LOOP structures from FORTRAN. After designing several Forth chips, he found that FOR-NEXT loop can be implemented as a single machine instruction. DO-LOOP structures were much too complicated to be reduced to hardware. This is the reason why eForth only has FOR-NEXT loop.

Memory Access

Four memory accessing words are included in the eForth kernel: !, @, C! and C@. ! and @ access memory in cells, whose size depends on the CPU underneath. eForth assumes that the CPU can access memory in bytes and that all addresses are in the units of bytes.

Porting eForth into a cell addressing CPU, C! and C@ must used
synthesized byte addresses and one must be able to switch between
cell addresses and byte addresses conveniently.

```
$CODE       1,'!',STORE     ! ( w a -- ) Pop the data stack to
                            memory.
POP         EBX             pop address a
POP         0[EBX]          pop w and store it in a
$NEXT

$CODE       1,'@',AT        @ ( a -- w ) Push memory location to
                            the data stack.
POP         EBX             pop address a
PUSH        0[EBX]          push contents of a
$NEXT

$CODE       2,'C!',CSTOR    C! ( c b -- ) Pop the data stack to byte
                            memory.
POP         EBX             pop address b
POP         EAX             pop byte c
MOV         0[EBX],AL       store c in b
$NEXT

$CODE       2,'C@',CAT      C@ ( b -- c ) Push byte memory location
                            to the data stack.
POP         EBX             pop address b
XOR         EAX,EAX         clear EAX to receive one byte
MOV         AL,0[EBX]       get one byte c at b
PUSH        EAX             push c
$NEXT
```

@ and C@ allow you to inspect any memory location in the
computer, and they can be executed harmlessly. On the other hand, !
and C! are dangerous. You can mistakenly store wrong data into the
dictionary, you variable area, and the stack area. When this happens,
most likely the Forth system will crash, or behave erratically.
However, it is very easy to reboot the system ans start over again. If
one develops a system incrementally and saves the source code
often, crashes do not seriously impede progress.

Return Stack

Return stack is used by the Virtual Forth Engine to save return
addresses in a token list to be processes later. It is also a convenient
place to store data temporarily. The return stack can thus be
considered as a extension of the data stack. However, one must be
very careful in using the return stack for temporary storage. The data
pushed on the return stack must be popped off before EXIT is
executed. Otherwise, EXIT will get the wrong address to return to,
and the system generally will crash.

RP@ and RP! are only used to initialize the return stack and are
seldom used in applications.

```
$CODE    3,'rp@',RPAT          RP@ ( -- a ) Push the current
                               RP on the data stack.
PUSH     EBP                   push RP on stack
$NEXT

$CODE    COMPO+3,'rp!',RPSTO   RP! ( a -- ) Set the return
                               stack pointer.
POP      EBP                   pop a and store it in RP
$NEXT
```

>R pops a number off the data stack and pushes it on the return
stack. R> does the opposite. R@ copies the top item on the return
stack and pushes it on the data stack, without disturbing the return
stack.

```
$CODE    2,'R>',RFROM          R> ( -- w ) Pop the return stack to the
                               data stack.
PUSH     0[EBP]                push top of return stack on data stack
ADD      EBP,CELLL             adjust RP
$NEXT

$CODE    2,'R@',RAT            R@ ( -- w ) Copy top of return stack to
                               the data stack.
PUSH     0[EBP]                push top of return stack on data stack
$NEXT                          leave RP alone
```

```
$CODE    COMPO+2,'>R',TOR    >R ( w -- ) Push the data stack to the
                             return stack.
SUB      EBP,CELLL           adjust RP
POP      0[EBP]              pop w and store it on return stack
$NEXT
```

Data Stack

Data stack is initialized by SP!. The depth of data stack can be examined by SP@. These words, as RP@ and RP! are only used by the system to initialize the data stack and very rarely used in applications. These words are necessary in the Forth kernel because you cannot operate a stack-based computer without these instructions. However, in a true Forth engine like NC4000 and RTX2000 which had build-in circular stacks in independent memory spaces, which were completely separated from the main memory, these stack words are unnecessary.

```
$CODE    3,'sp@',SPAT        sp@ ( -- a ) Push the current data
                             stack pointer.
MOV      EAX,ESP             Get data stack pointer ESP
PUSH     EAX                 Push it
$NEXT

$CODE    3,'sp!',SPSTO       sp! ( a -- ) Set the data stack pointer.
POP      EAX                 Pop a
MOV      ESP,EAX             Store it in ESP
$NEXT
```

In true Forth engines, we can eliminate these four instructions. However, to impose Virtual Forth Engines on conventional CPU's, we have to retain them to manage the stacks. It is very awkward to justify their existence in the eForth kernel since they do occupy 4 words among the 31 primitive eForth words, but are rarely used in applications.

The data stack is the centralized location where all numerical data are processed, and where parameters are passed from one word to another. The stack items have to be arranged properly so that they can be retrieved properly in the Last-In-First-Out (LIFO) manner.

When stack items are out of order, they can be rearranged by the stack words DUP, SWAP, OVER and DROP. There are other stack words useful in manipulating stack items, but these four are considered to be the minimum set.

```
$CODE    4,'DROP',DROP      DROP ( w -- ) Discard top stack item.
POP      EAX                pop it
$NEXT

$CODE    3,'DUP',DUPP       DUP ( w -- w w ) Duplicate the top stack
                            item.
POP      EAX                pop w
PUSH     EAX                push w twice
PUSH     EAX
$NEXT

$CODE    4,'SWAP',SWAP      SWAP ( w1 w2 -- w2 w1 ) Exchange top
                            two stack items.
POP      EBX                pop w2
POP      EAX                pop w1
PUSH     EBX                push w2
PUSH     EAX                push w1
$NEXT

$CODE    4,'OVER',OVER      OVER ( w1 w2 -- w1 w2 w1 ) Copy
                            second stack item to top.
MOV      EAX, 4[ESP]        get w1
PUSH     EAX                push w1
$NEXT
```

In this eForth Model, we use the system stack as the data stack. We can use the machine instructions PUSH and POP to access the data stack. Because 80x86 is a register-based CPU, all arithmetic and logic operations are performed in the CPU registers, it is necessary to POP items from the data stack into the registers for these operations, and then PUSH the results back on the data stack. This is the overhead we have to pay in using a register machine to emulate a stack machine.

Logic

The only primitive word which cares about logic is ?BRANCH. It tests the top item on the stack. If it is zero, ?BRANCH will branch to the following address. If it is not zero, ?BRANCH will ignore the address and execute the token after the branch address. Thus we distinguish two classes of numbers, zero for 'false' and non-zero for 'true'. Numbers used this way are called logic flags which can be either true or false. The only primitive word which generates flags is 0<, which examines the top item on the data stack for its negativeness. If it is negative, 0< will return a -1 for true. If it is 0 or positive, 0< will return a 0 for false.

```
$CODE    2,'0<',ZLESS    0< ( n -- t ) Return true if n is negative.
POP      EAX             pop n
CDQ                      sign extend EAX to EDX
PUSH     EDX             push sign as flag
$NEXT
```

The three logic words AND, OR and XOR are bitwise logic operators over the width of a cell. They can be used to operate on real flags (0 and -1) for logic purposes. You must be aware of the distinct behaviors between the real flags and the generalized flags.

```
$CODE    3,'AND',ANDD    AND ( w w -- w ) Bitwise AND.
POP      EAX
POP      EBX
AND      EAX,EBX         AND
PUSH     EAX
$NEXT

$CODE    2,'OR',ORR      OR ( w w -- w ) Bitwise inclusive OR.
POP      EAX
POP      EBX
OR       EAX,EBX         OR
PUSH     EAX
$NEXT

$CODE    3,'XOR',XORR    XOR( w w -- w ) Bitwise exclusive OR.
POP      EAX
```

```
POP      EBX
XOR      EAX,EBX          XOR
PUSH     EAX
$NEXT
```

Arithmetic

The only primitive arithmetic word in the eForth kernel is UM+. All other arithmetic words, like +, -, * and / are colon words derived from UM+ and some logic words. Bill Muench pioneered this design in his bForth. This design emphasize portability over performance, because it greatly reduces the efforts in moving eForth into CPU's which do not have native multiply and divide instructions. Once eForth is implemented on a new CPU, the multiply and divide words are the first ones to be optimized to enhance the performance.

UM+ adds two unsigned number on the top of the data stack and returns to the data stack the sum of these two numbers and the carry as one number on top of the sum. To handle the carry this way is very inefficient, because most CPU's have carry as a bit in the status register, and the carry can be accessed by many machine instructions. It is thus more convenient to use carry in machine code programming. eForth provides you a handle on the carry in high level, making it easier for you to deal with it directly.

Since it is slower to handle the carry in high level code, we expect that you will enhance the eForth system by recoding many of the high level ALU words in assembly so that the eForth system can run faster in real applications.

```
$CODE    3,'UM+',UPLUS    UM+ ( w w -- w cy ) Add two numbers,
                          return the sum and carry flag.
XOR      ECX,ECX          ECX=0 initial carry flag
POP      EBX
POP      EAX
ADD      EAX,EBX          ADD
RCL      ECX,1            get carry
PUSH     EAX              push sum
PUSH     ECX              push carry
$NEXT
```

Chapter 7. - Common Forth Words

Following are the eForth words originally defined as high level colon words. They are built from the primitive eForth words and other high level eForth words, including data structures and control structures. Since 86eForth v1.0 model was coded in Microsoft MASM assembler, the token lists in the colon words were constructed as data in MASM, using the DW directive. This form of representation, though very effective, is very difficult to read. The original model of eForth as provided by Bill Muench was in the form of a Forth source listing. This listing was much simpler and easy to read, assuming that the reader has some knowledge of the Forth syntax. This listing was also a very good source to learn a good coding style of Forth. I therefore thought it ws better to present the high level Forth colon words in this form. As the 86eForth v1.0 implementation deviates slightly from the original Forth model, I tried to translate the 8086 implementation faithfully back to the Forth style in the earlier editions of this book.

In this edition, I decided to follow faithfully the MASM source code, and all colon words are assembled as token lists with DD directives, as all tokens are 4 bytes in length. Hence I do not have to assume that you have prior knowledge of Forth programming language and its unique syntax. Only MASM assembly language and 80x86 instruction set are required to read this book.

Another major deviation from 86eForth v1.0 is that all colon words that can be optimized are re-coded in 80x86 assembly. Number of code words are increased from 31 to 71. They are very good assembly programming examples if you are learning 80x86 processors.

The sequence of words is exactly the same as that in the MASM assembly source listing. You are encouraged to read the MASM source listing along with the text in this book. Reading two descriptions of the same subject often enable better comprehension and understanding.

System Variables

The term user variable was codified in earlier Forth systems on the mini-computers in which multitasking was an integral part of the Forth operating system. In a multitasking system, many users share one CPU and other resources in the computing system. Each user has a private memory area to store essential information about its own task so that the system can leave a task temporarily to serve other users and return to this task continuing the unfinished work. In a single user environment, user variables are simply system variables.

In 86eForth v5.2, system variables are reduced to 13, and are place in the beginning of .data segment, as discussed earlier. A special memory area in the high memory is allocated for all these variables, and they are all initialized by copying a table of initial values stored in the cold boot area. A significant benefit of this scheme is that it allows the eForth system to operate in ROM memory naturally. It is very convenient for embedded system applications which preclude mass storage and file downloading.

```
$CODE    3,'sp0',SZERO        SP0 ( -- a ) Pointer to bottom of
                              the data stack.
LEA      EAX,_SPP             bottom of data stack
PUSH     EAX                  push
$NEXT

$CODE    3,'rp0',RZERO        RP0 ( -- a ) Pointer to bottom of
                              the return stack.
LEA      EAX,_RPP             bottom of return stack
PUSH     EAX                  push
$NEXT

$CODE    4,'base',BASE        BASE ( -- a ) Storage of the
                              radix base for numeric I/O.
LEA      EAX,_BASE            Radix for number conversion
PUSH     EAX
$NEXT

$CODE    COMPO+3,'tmp',TEMP   TMP ( -- a ) Temporary storage
                              location used in parse and find.
LEA      EAX,_TMP             Temporary storage
PUSH     EAX
```

```
$NEXT

$CODE    4,'span',SPAN              SPAN ( -- a ) Hold character
                                    count received by EXPECT.
LEA      EAX,_SPAN                  Character count received
PUSH     EAX
$NEXT

$CODE    3,'>in',INN                >IN ( -- a ) Character pointer
                                    while parsing input stream.
LEA      EAX,_IN                    Parser pointer
PUSH     EAX
$NEXT

$CODE    4,'#tib',NTIB              #TIB ( -- a ) Hold the current
                                    count the terminal input buffer.
LEA      EAX,_NTIB                  Pointer to end of input buffer
PUSH     EAX
$NEXT

$CODE    3,'hld',HLD                HLD ( -- a ) Pointer to numeric
                                    output string under
                                    construction.
LEA      EAX,_HLD                   Pointer to output number string
PUSH     EAX
$NEXT

$CODE    3,"'eval",TEVAL            'EVAL ( -- a ) Hold
                                    $INTERPRET or $COMPILE.
LEA      EAX,_EVAL                  Execution vector for text
                                    interpreter
PUSH     EAX
$NEXT

$CODE    7,'context',CNTXT          CONTEXT ( -- a ) Pointer to
                                    last name in dictionary.
LEA      EAX,_CNTXT                 Pointer to last name
PUSH     EAX
$NEXT

$CODE    2,'cp',CP                  CP ( -- a ) Pointer to the top of
                                    the code dictionary.
LEA      EAX,_CP                    Pointer to top of dictionary
PUSH     EAX
$NEXT

$CODE    4,'last',LAST              LAST ( -- a ) Pointer to the last
```

```
                                          name in dictionary.
LEA        EAX,_LASTN                     Initial value for CONTEXT
PUSH       EAX
$NEXT
```

More Stack Words

This group of stack words are commonly used in writing Forth applications. They are originally coded in high level to enhance the portability. In this 86eForth v5.2 implementations, they are mostly coded in machine language to increase the execute speed. They supplement the four classic stack operators DUP, SWAP, OVER and DROP.

?DUP duplicates the top of stack only if it is not zero. It is very useful when we are interested in the value of a number to do some useful things. If it is zero, it will not be used and then dropped. Why duplicate it if we will not use it? However, it is problematic, because it changes the depth of data stack. In most circumstances, we would expect that the data stack is balance, and ?DUP is an exception.

```
        $CODE    4,'?DUP',QDUP      ?DUP ( w — w w | 0 ) Dup
                                    tos if it is not zero.
        POP      EAX
        OR       EAX,EAX            test tos
        JZ       SHORT QDUP1
        PUSH     EAX                push twice
QDUP1:  PUSH     EAX                push once
        $NEXT
```

ROT is unique in that it accesses the third item on the data stack. All other stack operators can only access one or two stack items. In Forth programming, it is generally accepted that one should not try to access stack items deeper than the third item. When you have to dig deep into the stack, the code becomes very difficult to read because of all the stack operations. This is one of the reasons why Forth acquired the reputation of a write-only language. Proper factoring is the best cure against this tendency.

When you have to access deeper into the data stack, it is a good time to re-evaluate your algorithm. Most often, you can avoid this situation by factoring your code into smaller parts which do not reach so deep.

```
$CODE    3,'ROT',ROT        ROT ( w1 w2 w3 -- w2 w3 w1 ) Rotate
                            three item to top.
POP      EAX                pop all 3 items
POP      EBX
POP      ECX
PUSH     EBX                push them in desired order
PUSH     EAX
PUSH     ECX
$NEXT
```

2DUP and 2DROP are useful when you are manipulating double integers on stack.

```
$CODE    5,'2DROP',DDROP    2DROP ( w w -- ) Discard top two
                            items on stack.
POP      EAX
POP      EAX
$NEXT


$CODE    4,'2DUP',DDUP      2DUP ( w1 w2 -- w1 w2 w1 w2 )
                            Duplicate top two items.
POP      EAX                Pop w2
POP      EBX                Pop w1
PUSH     EBX                push w1
PUSH     EAX                push w2
PUSH     EBX                push w1
PUSH     EAX                push w2
$NEXT
```

More Arithmetic Words

In the 86eForth v1.0, this group of arithmetic operators are simple extensions from the primitive word UM+. It is interesting to see how the more commonly used arithmetic operators are derived. + is UM+ with the carry discarded. But, ADD is a 8086 machine instruction, and there is not reason not to take advantage of it.

```
$CODE     1,'+',PLUS      + ( w w -- sum ) Add top two items.
POP       EAX
POP       EBX
ADD       EAX,EBX         ADD
PUSH      EAX
$NEXT
```

D+ can also be expressed very easily in 8086 assembly.

```
$CODE     2,'D+',DPLUS    D+ ( d d -- d ) Double integer addition.
POP       EAX
POP       EDX
POP       EBX
POP       ECX
ADD       EDX,ECX         add lower half
ADC       EAX,EBX         add upper half with carry
PUSH      EDX             push lower sum
PUSH      EAX             push upper sum
$NEXT
```

NOT returns the ones compliment of a number, and NEGATE returns the two's compliment. Because UM+ preserves the carry, it can be used to form multiple precision operators like D+. Later we will see how UM+ is used to do multiplication and division.

```
$CODE      3,'NOT',INVER          NOT ( w -- w ) One's
                                  complement of tos.
POP        EAX
NOT        EAX                    invert all bits
PUSH       EAX
$NEXT


$CODE      6,'NEGATE',NEGAT       NEGATE ( n -- -n ) Two's
                                  complement of tos.
POP        EAX
NEG        EAX                    negate
PUSH       EAX
$NEXT
```

In this 86eForth v5.2, most of these words are code words, because 80x86 CPU has these functions in its instruction set. All we have to do is popping data from data stack into the proper registers and let CPU do the work. These code words, DNEGATE, - and ABS are good examples in 80x86 assembly programming.

```
$CODE      7,'DNEGATE',DNEGA      DNEGATE ( d -- -d )
                                  Two's complement of
                                  top double integer.
POP        EAX                    dh
POP        EDX                    dl
NEG        EAX                    negate dh
NEG        EDX                    negate dl
SBB        EAX,0                  Carry into dh
PUSH       EDX
PUSH       EAX
$NEXT


$CODE      1,'-',SUBBB            - ( n1 n2 -- n1-n2 )
                                  Subtraction.
POP        EBX
POP        EAX
SUB        EAX,EBX                SUB
PUSH       EAX
$NEXT


$CODE      3,'ABS',ABSS           ABS ( n -- n ) Return the
                                  absolute value of n.
POP        EAX
OR         EAX,EAX
```

```
          JGE       SHORT ABS1          Positive?
          NEG       EAX                 negative
ABS1:     PUSH      EAX
          $NEXT
```

More Comparison Words

'=' (Equal) compares top two numbers on data stack. It returns a true flag if these numbers are equal. Otherwise it returns a false flag. The command '-' serves well for this function, if you will use a non-zero number as a true flag. To adhere to a more restrictive definition of true flag as -1, you have to use '='.

```
          $CODE     1,'=',EQUAL         = ( w w -- t ) Return true if top
                                        two are equal.
          XOR       EAX,EAX             init a false flag
          POP       EDX
          POP       EBX
          XOR       EDX,EBX             compare
          JNZ       SHORT EQU1
          DEC       EAX                 change false flag to true flag
EQU1:     PUSH      EAX
          $NEXT
```

U< is used to compared two unsigned numbers. This operator is very important, especially in comparing addresses, as we assume that the addresses are unsigned numbers pointing to unique memory locations. The arithmetic comparison operator < cannot be used to determine whether one address is higher or lower than the other. Using < for address comparison had been the single cause of many failures in the annals of Forth.

```
          $CODE     2,'U<',ULESS        U< ( u u -- t ) Unsigned
                                        compare of top two items.
          POP       EBX
          POP       EAX
          SUB       EAX,EBX             compare
          SBB       EAX,EAX             use carry to generate true
```

```
                                        or false flag
              PUSH      EAX
              $NEXT

              $CODE     1,'<',LESS      < ( n1 n2 -- t ) Signed
                                        compare of top two items.
              XOR       EAX,EAX         init false flag
              POP       EBX
              POP       ECX
              SUB       ECX,EBX         compare
              JGE       SHORT LESS1
              DEC       EAX             make true flag
      LESS1:  PUSH      EAX
              $NEXT
```

MAX retains the larger of the top two items on the data stack. Both numbers are assumed to be signed integers.

```
              $CODE     3,'MAX',MAX     MAX ( n n -- n ) Return the
                                        greater of two top stack
                                        items.
              POP       EBX
              POP       EAX
              CMP       EAX,EBX         compare
              JGE       SHORT MAX1      select larger
              XCHG      EAX,EBX
      MAX1:   PUSH      EAX
              $NEXT
```

MIN retains the smaller of the top two items on the data stack. Both numbers are assumed to be signed integers.

```
              $CODE     3,'MIN',MIN     MIN ( n n -- n ) Return the
                                        smaller of top two stack
                                        items.
              POP       EBX
              POP       EAX
              CMP       EAX,EBX         compare
              JGE       SHORT MIN1      select smaller
              XCHG      EAX,EBX
```

```
MIN1:   PUSH        EBX
        $NEXT
```

WITHIN checks whether the third item on the data stack is within the range as specified by the top two numbers on the data stack. The range is inclusive as to the lower limit and exclusive to the upper limit. If the third item is within range, a true flag is returned on the data stack. Otherwise, a false flag is returned. All numbers are assumed to be unsigned integers.

```
$COLON   6,'WITHIN',WITHI      WITHIN ( u ul uh -- t ) Return
                               true if u is within the range of ul
                               and uh.
DD       OVER,SUBBB,TOR        range between ul and uh
DD       SUBBB,RFROM,ULESS     range between ul and uh
DD       EXITT
```

Multiply and Divide

This group of words provides a variety of multiplication and division functions. In 86eForth v1.0, they are all based on the primitive UM+ operator in the kernel. Building this word set in high level has the penalty that all math operations will be slow. However, since Forth needs these functions only in numeric I/O conversions, the performance of eForth itself is not substantially affected by them. Nevertheless, if an application requires lots of numeric computations, a few critical words in this word set should be re-coded in assembly. The primary candidates for optimization are UM/MOD and UM*, because all other multiply and divide operators are derived from these two words.

In 86eForth v5.2, all these words which can be optimized are re-coded as code words.

UM/MOD and UM* are the most complicated and comprehensive division and multiplication operators. Once they are coded, all other division and multiplication operators can be derived easily. It has been a tradition in Forth coding that one solves the most difficult problem first, and all other problems are solved by themselves.

UM/MOD divides an unsigned double integer by an unsigned single integer. It returns the unsigned remainder and unsigned quotient on the data stack.

```
        $CODE   6,'UM/MOD',UMMOD   UM/MOD ( udl udh un --
                                   ur uq ) Unsigned divide
                                   of a double by a single.
                                   Return mod and
                                   quotient.
        POP     EBX                un
        POP     EDX                udh
        POP     EAX                udl
        OR      EBX,EBX            If un =0
        JNZ     SHORT UMM1         return two -1's
UMM:    MOV     EAX,-1
        PUSH    EAX
        PUSH    EAX
        $NEXT
UMM1:   DIV     EBX                else unsigned divide
        PUSH    EDX                remainder
        PUSH    EAX                quotient
        $NEXT
```

M/MOD divides a signed double integer by a signed single integer. It returns the signed remainder and signed quotient on the data stack. The signed division is floored towards negative infinity.

```
        $CODE   5,'M/MOD',MSMOD    M/MOD ( d n -- r q ) Signed
                                   floored divide of double by
                                   single. Return mod and
                                   quotient.
        POP     EBX                n
        POP     EDX                dh
        POP     EAX                dl
        OR      EBX,EBX            If n=0
        JZ      SHORT UMM          then, return two -1
MSM1:   DIV     EBX                signed divide
        PUSH    EDX                remainder
        PUSH    EAX                quotient
        $NEXT
```

/MOD divides a signed single integer by a signed integer. It returns the signed remainder and quotient.

```
$COLON   4,'/MOD',SLMOD      /MOD ( n1 n2 -- r q ) Signed divide.
                             Return mod and quotient.
DD       OVER,ZLESS,SWAP     sign extend n1
DD       MSMOD,EXITT         floored divide
```

MOD is similar to /MOD, except that only the signed remainder is returned.

```
$COLON   3,'MOD',MODD        MOD ( n n -- r ) Signed divide.
                             Return mod only.
DD       SLMOD,DROP,EXITT    divide and discard remainder
```

/ is also similar to /MOD, except that only the signed quotient is returned.

```
$COLON   1,'/',SLASH         / ( n n -- q ) Signed divide. Return
                             quotient only.
DD       SLMOD,SWAP,DROP     divide and discard quotient
DD       EXITT
```

UM* is the most complicated multiplication operation. Once it is coded, all other multiplication words can be derived from it.

UM* multiplies two unsigned single integers and returns the unsigned double integer product on the data stack.

```
$CODE    3,'UM*',UMSTA       UM* ( u u -- ud ) Unsigned multiply.
                             Return double product.
POP      EAX
POP      EBX
MUL      EBX                 unsigned multiply
PUSH     EAX
PUSH     EDX
$NEXT
```

M* multiplies two signed single integers and returns the signed double integer product on the data stack.

```
$CODE    2,'M*',MSTAR      M* ( n n -- d ) Signed multiply. Return
                           double product.
POP      EBX
POP      EAX
IMUL     EBX              signed multiply
PUSH     EAX
PUSH     EDX
$NEXT
```

* multiplies two signed single integers and returns the signed single integer product on the data stack. Again, advanced CPU's generally have these multiplication operations as native machine instructions. You should take advantage of these resources to enhance the eForth
system.

```
$CODE    1,'*',STAR        * ( n n -- n ) Signed multiply. Return
                           single product.
POP      EAX
POP      EBX
IMUL     EBX              signed multiply
PUSH     EAX
$NEXT
```

Scaling

Forth is very close to the machine language that it generally only handles integer numbers. There are floating point extensions on many more sophisticated Forth systems, but they are more exceptions than rules. The reason that Forth has traditionally been an integer language is that integers are handled faster and more efficiently in the computers, and most technical problems can be solved satisfactorily using integers only. A 16-bit integer has the dynamic range of 110 dB which is far more than enough for most engineering problems. The precision of a 16-bit integer representation is limited to one part in 65535, which could be inadequate for small numbers. However, the precision can be greatly improved by scaling; i.e., taking the ratio of two integers. It was demonstrated that pi, or any other irrational numbers, can be represented accurately to 1 part in 100,000,000 by a ratio of two 16-bit integers.

The scaling operators */MOD and */ are useful in scaling number n1 by the ratio of n2/n3. When n2 and n3 are properly chosen, the scaling operation can preserve precision similar to the floating point operations at a much higher speed. Notice also that in these scaling operations, the intermediate product of n1 and n2 is a double precision integer so that the precision of scaling is maintained.

$COLON	5,'*/MOD',SSMOD	*/MOD (n1 n2 n3 -- r q) Multiply n1 and n2, then divide by n3. Return mod and quotient.
DD	TOR,MSTAR	n1*n2
DD	RFROM,MSMOD,EXITT	n1*n2/n3 with remainder
$COLON	2,'*/',STASL	*/ (n1 n2 n3 -- q) Multiply n1 by n2, then divide by n3. Return quotient only.
DD	SSMOD,SWAP	n1*n2/n3
DD	DROP,EXITT	discard remainder

Memory Alignment Words

The most serious problem in porting system from one computer to another is that different computers have different sizes for their addresses and data. We generally classify computers as 8, 16, 32-bit machines, because they operate on data of these various sizes. It is thus difficult to port a single programming model as eForth to all these computers. In eForth, a set of memory alignment words helps to make it easier to port the same eForth model to different machines.

We assume that the target computer can address it memory in 8 bit chunks (bytes). The natural width of data best handled by the computer is thus a multiple of bytes. A unit of such data is a cell. A

16 bit machine handles data in 2 byte cells, and a 32 bit machine handles data in 4 byte cells.

4+ increments the memory address by the cell size in bytes, and 4- decrements the memory address by the cell size. 4* multiplies the cell number on the stack by 4. These words are very useful in converting a cell offset into a byte offset, in order to access integers in a data array.

```
$CODE    2,'4+',CELLP    4+ ( a -- a+4 ) Add cell size in byte to
                         address.
POP      EAX
ADD      EAX,CELLL       plus 4
PUSH     EAX
$NEXT


$CODE    2,'4-',CELLM    4- ( a -- a-4 ) Subtract cell size in byte
                         from address.
POP      EAX
SUB      EAX,CELLL       minus 4
PUSH     EAX
$NEXT


$CODE    2,'4*',CELLS    4* ( n -- 4n ) Multiply tos by cell size in
                         bytes.
POP      EAX
SHL      EAX,2           shift left 2 bits
PUSH     EAX
$NEXT
```

In building the text interpreter and compiler, we often have to modify an address or an address offset on top of stack to access data in the neighborhood of this address. In this 32-bit Forth system, we need to increment or decrement the address by 1, 2, or 4, and we also need to multiply an address offset by 4. Having a set of incrementing, decrementing and bit shifting words reduces the size of compiled code and speed up computing.

```
$CODE    2,'1+',ONEP    1+ ( a -- a+1 ) Add cell size in byte to address.
POP      EAX
ADD      EAX,1          increment
PUSH     EAX
```

```
$NEXT
```

$CODE	2,'1-',ONEM	1- (a -- a-1) Subtract cell size in byte from address.
POP	EAX	
SUB	EAX,1	decrement
PUSH	EAX	
$NEXT		

$CODE	2,'2+',TWOP	2+ (a -- a+2) Add cell size in byte to address.
POP	EAX	
ADD	EAX,2	increment by 2
PUSH	EAX	
$NEXT		

$CODE	2,'2-',TWOM	2- (a -- a+2) Subtract cell size in byte from address.
POP	EAX	
SUB	EAX,2	Decrement by 2
PUSH	EAX	
$NEXT		

Special Characters

The blank character (ASCII 32) is special in eForth because it is the most often used character to delimit words in the input stream and the most often used character to format the output strings. It is used so often that it is advantageous to define a unique word for it. BL simply returns the number 32 on the data stack.

$COLON	2,'BL',BLANK	BL (-- 32) Return 32, the blank character.
DD	DOLIT,' ',EXITT	blank

>CHAR is very important in converting a non-printable character to a harmless 'underscore' character (ASCII 95). As eForth is designed to communicate with you through a serial I/O device, it is important that eForth will not emit control characters to the host and causes unexpected behavior on the host computer. >CHAR thus filters the characters before they are sent out by TYPE.

```
        $COLON  5,'>char',TCHAR              >CHAR ( c -- c )
                                             Filter non-
                                             printing
                                             characters.
        DD      DOLIT,07FH,ANDD,DUPP         mask msb
        DD      DOLIT,127,BLANK,WITHI        check for
                                             printable
        DD      QBRAN,TCHA1
        DD      DROP,DOLIT,'_'               replace non-
                                             printable
TCHA1:
        DD      EXITT
```

Managing Data Stack

The data stack is one of the most important resources in a Forth system. You has to have the complete knowledge of what's on the stack in order to be sure that your program is operating properly. The Forth words discussed so far allows you to access only the top 3 items on the stack. In coding small modules, you are not expected to access stack items more than 3 levels deep. However, in running significant applications, there are occasions when you have to reach deeper into the stack.

In 86eForth v1.0, there was a utility word .S which dumps non-destructively the contents of the data stack for you to examine. The stack words DEPTH and PICK are included in the eForth system mainly to support this stack dump utility. However, in 86eForth v5.2, .S is changed to show only the top 4 elements on the stack. It is used to show the stack after lines of input is interpreted successfully. When top 4 elements on the stack is always visible, it is not necessary to dump the stack.

DEPTH returns the number of items currently on the data stack. PICK takes a number n off the data stack and replaces it with the n'th item on the data stack. The number n is 0-based; i.e., the top item is number 0, the next item is number 1, etc. Therefore, 0 PICK is equivalent to DUP, and 1 PICK is equivalent to OVER.

$COLON	5,'depth',DEPTH	**DEPTH (-- n) Return the depth of the data stack.**
DD	SPAT,DOLIT,_SPP,AT	**top and bottom of data stack**
DD	SWAP,SUBBB	
DD	DOLIT,CELLL,SLASH	**divide by 4**
DD	EXITT	
$COLON	4,'PICK',PICK	**PICK (.. +n -- .. w) Copy the nth stack item to tos.**
DD	ONEP,CELLS	**0 based**
DD	SPAT,PLUS,AT,EXITT	**reach into data stack**

As discussed in an earlier section, DUP, SWAP, OVER and ROT should be able to handle most situations in Forth programming. If you find yourself in a situation that you have to use PICK, something is wrong and you should look more carefully in your code to see if there are ways to simplify your code.

Memory Access

There are three useful memory operators. +! increments the contents of a memory location by an integer on the stack.

$CODE	2,'+!',PSTOR	**+! (n a --) Add n to the contents at address a.**
POP	EBX	**a**
POP	EAX	**n**
ADD	0[EBX],EAX	**add n to [a]**
$NEXT		

2! and 2@ store and fetch double integers to and from memory.

$CODE	2,'2!',DSTOR	**2! (d a --) Store the double integer to address a.**
POP	EBX	
POP	0[EBX]	**dl**
POP	4[EBX]	**dh**
$NEXT		

```
$CODE    2,'2@',DAT        2@ ( a -- d ) Fetch double integer from
                           address a.
POP      EBX
PUSH     4[EBX]            dh
PUSH     0[EBX]            dl
$NEXT
```

There are three buffer areas used often in the eForth system. HERE returns the address of the first free location above the code dictionary, where new words are compiled. PAD returns the address of the text buffer where numbers are constructed and text strings are stored temporarily. TIB is the terminal input buffer where input text string is held.

```
$COLON   4,'HERE',HERE     HERE ( -- a ) Return the top of the
                           code dictionary.
DD       CP,AT,EXITT       [cp]

$COLON   3,'PAD',PAD       PAD ( -- a ) Return the address of
                           the text buffer above the code
                           dictionary.
DD       HERE,DOLIT,80     [cp]+80
DD       PLUS,EXITT

$COLON   3,'TIB',TIB       TIB ( -- a ) Return the address of the
                           terminal input buffer.
DD       DOLIT,_TIB,EXITT  terminal input buffer
```

@EXECUTE is a special word supporting the vectored execution words in eForth. It fetches the code field address of a token and executes the token.

```
$COLON   8,'@EXECUTE',ATEXE  @EXECUTE ( a -- )
                             Execute vector
                             stored in address a.
DD       AT,QDUP             address or zero?
DD       QBRAN,EXE1
DD       EXECU               execute if non-zero
```

```
EXE1:
         DD      EXITT                    do nothing if zero
```

Array and String Words

A memory array is generally specified by a starting address and its length in bytes. In a string, the first byte is a count byte, specifying the number of bytes in the following string. This is called a counted string. String literals in the colon words and the name strings in the name fields of word records are all represented by counted strings. Following are special words which handles memory arrays and strings.

COUNT converts a string array address to the address-length representation of a counted string.

```
$CODE   5,'COUNT',COUNT      COUNT ( b -- b+1 c ) Return count
                             byte of a string and add 1 to byte
                             address.
POP     EBX                  get b
XOR     EAX,EAX              clear EAX to receive one byte
MOV     AL,0[EBX]            get c
INC     EBX                  increment b
PUSH    EBX                  push b+1
PUSH    EAX                  push c
$NEXT
```

CMOVE copies a memory array from one location to another. 8086 CPU has very powerful byte movement instruction I can take advantage of. REP MOVSB copies a byte array from one place to another.

```
$CODE      5,'CMOVE',CMOVEE    CMOVE ( b1 b2 u -- ) Copy u
                               bytes from b1 to b2.
MOV        EBX,ESI             save IP
POP        ECX                 get count
POP        EDI
POP        ESI
REP  MOVSB                     repeat move bytes
MOV        ESI,EBX             restore IP
$NEXT
```

FILL fills a memory array with the same byte. . 8086 CPU has very powerful byte storage instruction. REP STOSB initializes a byte array.

```
$CODE        4,'FILL',FILL      FILL ( b u c -- ) Fill u bytes of
                                character c to area beginning at
                                b.
POP          EAX                get byte pattern c
POP          ECX                get count u
POP          EDI                get address b
REP STOSB                       repeat store bytes
$NEXT
```

ERASE fills a memory area with 0 bytes.

```
$COLON       5,'ERASE',ERASE    ERASE ( b u -- ) Erase u bytes
                                beginning at b.
DD           DOLIT,0,FILL        just fill with 0
DD           EXITT
```

Arrays and strings are generally specified by the address of the first byte in the array or string, and the byte length. This specification of course is the consequence that the memory is byte addressable. In a CPU which addresses memory in cells, these words must be defined in terms of an artificial byte space.

PACK$ is an important string handling word used by the text interpreter. It copies a text string from one location to another. In the target area, the string is converted to a counted string by adding a count byte before the text of the string. This word is used to build the name field of a new word at the top of the dictionary. PACK$ is designed so that it can pack bytes into cells in a cell addressable machine.

$COLON	5, 'pack$', PACKS	**PACK$ (b u a -- a) Build a counted at a from string with u characters at b.**
DD	DUPP, TOR	save count
DD	DDUP, CSTOR, ONEP	store count
DD	SWAP, CMOVEE, RFROM	move string
DD	EXITT	

In 86eForth v1.0, headers and code fields are aligned to 2-byte word cells. Earlier 32-bit 86eForth implementation aligned headers fields to 4-byte cell boundaries, which was wasteful. In the current 86eForth v5.2, I take advantage of the fact that 80x86 CPU does not require machine instructions or data to be aligned to cell boundaries. Therefore, link fields, name fields, code fields and parameter fields fall to wherever address on assembling. New words compiled into the .data segment are not aligned either. PACK$ does not align the counted string in target location. The price we pay for not aligning strings is that when we have to compare names of commands in SAME?, the comparison must be done byte-by byte, not 4 bytes at a time.

A cheap way to implement eForth on a cell addressable machine is to equate cell addresses to byte addresses, and to store one byte in a cell. This scheme is workable, but very inefficient in memory utilization. PACK$ is a tool which helps you bridging the gap.

Chapter 8. - Text Interpreter

The text interpreter is also called the outer interpreter in Forth. It is functionally equivalent to an operating system in a conventional computer. It accepts commands similar to English you entered on a keyboard, and carries out the tasks specified by the commands. As an operating system, the text interpreter must be complicated, because of all the things it has to do. However, because Forth employs very simple syntax rules, and has very simple internal structures, the Forth text interpreter is much simpler that conventional operating systems. It is simple enough that we can discuss it completely in a single chapter, admittedly that this is a long chapter.

Let us summarize what a text interpreter must do in a flowchart-like diagram:

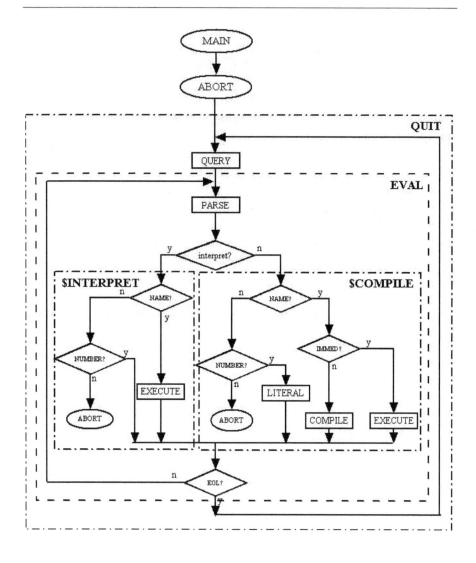

The goal of the text interpreter is to accept a line of Forth commands from a terminal, execute these commands in sequence, and wait for another line of commands. As shown in the flowchart shown above, all Forth commands are enclosed in rectangles, big and small. Diamonds show decision making words. Lines with arrows show sequences of operation. As we go through source code in 86eForth502.asm line by line, you will see how these commands are implemented, and will appreciate the overall design of this 86eForth v5.2 system.

Let us summarize the function of individual words in the text interpreter:

MAIN	Set up Virtual Forth Engine
COLD	Initialize system variables
ABORT	Reset data stack. Error handler
QUIT	Reset return stack and enter interpreter loop
QUERY	Accept text input from a terminal
EVAL	Evaluate or interpret a line of text
PARSE	Parse out a word from input text
$INTERPRET	Interpret a word
$COMPILE	Compile a word
NAME$	Search dictionary for a word
NUMBER?	Translate a text string into an integer
EXECUTE	Execute a word
IMMED?	Is this word an immediate command?
LITERAL	Compile a integer literal
COMPILE	Compile a token

In the assembly source code, we will build and integrate these functions gradually in modules. All modules finally fall into their places in the command QUIT, which is the text interpreter itself.

You might want to look up the code of QUIT first and see how the modules fit together. A good feeling for the big picture will help you in understanding lower modules. Nevertheless, we will doggedly follow the loading order in the source code, and hope that you will not get lost in the process.

Numeric Output

Forth is interesting in its special capabilities in handling numbers across the man-machine interface. It recognizes that the machine and the human prefer very different representations of numbers. The machine prefers a binary representation, but the human prefers decimal Arabic digital representations. However, depending on circumstances, you may want numbers to be represented in other radices, like hexadecimal, octal, and sometimes binary.

Forth solves this problem of internal (machine) versus external (human) number representations by insisting that all numbers are represented in the binary form in the CPU and in memory. Only when numbers are imported or exported for human consumption are they converted to the external ASCII representation. The radix of external representation is controlled by the radix value stored in the variable BASE.

Since BASE is a system variable, you can select any reasonable radix for entering numbers into the computer and formatting numbers to be shown to you. Most programming languages can handle a small set of radices, like decimal, octal, hexadecimal and binary, with explicit prefix or postfix characters. In Forth, radix for number conversion is implicit, stored in BASE. It had caused endless grieves, even to very experience Forth programmers, because one did not know the true value of a number without knowing what was in BASE at the moment.

BASE is one of the very important inventions by Chuck Moore who gave us the Forth language. It gives us freedom of expression, in representing numbers any way we choose for whatever the reason at the moment.

In the following figure, I try to show you how input numbers are converted from external to internal representation and how output numbers are converted from internal to external representation.

DIGIT converts an integer to a digit.

```
$COLON    5,'digit',DIGIT          DIGIT ( u -- c ) Convert digit
                                   u to a character.
DD        DOLIT,9,OVER,LESS        If u>9,
DD        DOLIT,7,ANDD,PLUS        add 7 for a hex number.
DD        DOLIT,'0',PLUS,EXITT     convert to ASCII
```

EXTRACT extracts the least significant digit from a number n. n is divided by the radix in BASE and returned on the stack.

```
$COLON    7,'extract',EXTRC    EXTRACT ( n base -- n c )
                               Extract the least significant digit
                               from n.
DD        DOLIT,0,SWAP,UMMOD   extract least significant digit
DD        SWAP,DIGIT,EXITT     convert to ASCII digit
```

Number Formatting

The output number string is built below the PAD buffer. The least significant digit is extracted from an integer on the top of data stack by dividing it by the current radix in BASE. One digit thus extracted is added to the output string backwards from PAD to lower memory. The conversion is terminated when the integer is divided to zero. The address and length of the number string are made available by #> for outputting.

The following figure show how a number 123456 on top of parameter stack is converted to a number string 123456 in the number buffer, ready to be typed out to a terminal:

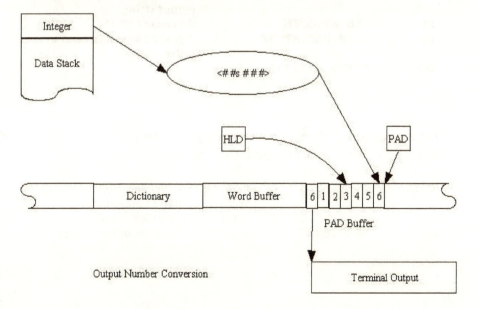

Output Number Conversion

An output number conversion is initiated by <# and terminated by #>. Between them, # converts one digit at a time, #S converts all the digits, while HOLD and SIGN inserts special characters into the string under construction. This set of tokens is very versatile and can handle many different output formats.

<# initiates the output number conversion process by storing PAD buffer address into variable HLD, which points to the location next numeric digit will be stored.

$COLON	2,'<#',BDIGS	<# (--) **Initiate the numeric output process.**
DD	PAD,HLD,STORE	**point HLD to PAD to accept numeric digits**
DD	EXITT	

HOLD appends an ASCII character whose code is on the top of the parameter stack, to the numeric output string at HLD. HLD is decremented to receive the next digit.

$COLON	4,'HOLD',HOLD	HOLD (c --) **Insert a character into the numeric output string.**
DD	HLD,AT,ONEM	**decrement HLD**
DD	DUPP,HLD,STORE	**digits are stored in reverse order**
DD	CSTOR,EXITT store digit c	

extracts one digit from integer on the top of the parameter stack, according to radix in BASE, and add it to output numeric string.

$COLON	1,'#',DIG	# (u -- u) **Extract one digit from u and append the digit to output string.**
DD	BASE,AT,EXTRC	**extract least significant digit**
DD	HOLD,EXITT	**append it to numeric output string**

#S extracts all digits to output string until the integer on the top of the parameter stack is divided down to 0.

```
        $COLON   2,'#S',DIGS    #S ( u -- 0 ) Convert u until
                                all digits are added to the
                                output string.
DIGS1:  DD       DIG,DUPP       append one digit
        DD       QBRAN,DIGS2    If u is not 0,
        DD       BRAN,DIGS1     repeat until u is reduced to 0
DIGS2:  DD       EXITT
```

SIGN inserts a - sign into the numeric output string if the integer on the top of the parameter stack is negative.

```
        $COLON   4,'SIGN',SIGN  SIGN ( n -- ) Add a minus
                                sign to the numeric output
                                string.
        DD       ZLESS          If n<0,
        DD       QBRAN,SIGN1
        DD       DOLIT,'-',HOLD append minus sign
SIGN1:  DD       EXITT
```

#> terminates the numeric conversion and pushes the address and length of output numeric string on the parameter stack.

```
$COLON   2,'#>',EDIGS   #> ( w -- b u ) Prepare the output string
                         to be TYPEed.
DD       DROP,HLD,AT     replace w with HLD
DD       PAD,OVER,SUBBB  return length of string
DD       EXITT
```

Number Output

With the number formatting word set as shown above, one can format numbers for output in any form desired. The free output format is a number string preceded by a single space. The fix column format displays a number right-justified in a column of predetermined width. The commands ., U., and ? use a free format. The commands .R and U.R use a fix format.

STR converts a signed integer on the top of data stack to a numeric output string.

$COLON	3,'str',STRR	str (w -- b u) Convert a signed integer to a numeric string.
DD	DUPP,TOR,ABSS	save w for SIGN, and change w to absolute
DD	BDIGS,DIGS,RFROM	extract all digits of absolute value
DD	SIGN,EDIGS,EXITT	append sign and return buffer and length

.R displays a signed integer n , the second item on the parameter stack, right-justified in a field of +n characters. +n is on the top of the parameter stack.

$COLON	2,'.R',DOTR	.R (w +n --) Display an integer in a field of n columns, right justified.
DD	TOR,STRR,RFROM	save column width +n and convert w
DD	OVER,SUBBB,SPACS	display spaces for right justification
DD	TYPES,EXITT	display number string

U.R displays an unsigned integer n right-justified in a field of +n characters.

$COLON	3,'U.R',UDOTR	U.R (w +n --) Display an unsigned integer in n column, right justified.
DD	TOR,BDIGS,DIGS,EDIGS	convert unsigned integer w
DD	RFROM,OVER,SUBBB,SPACS	add spaces for right justification
DD	TYPES,EXITT	display number string

U. displays an unsigned integer u in free format, followed by a space.

```
$COLON    2,'U.',UDOT         U. ( u -- ) Display an unsigned
                              integer in free format.
DD        BDIGS,DIGS,EDIGS    convert unsigned integer w
DD        SPACE,TYPES,EXITT   add space and display number
                              string
```

. (dot) displays a signed integer n in free format, followed by a space.

```
$COLON    1,'.',DOT                      . ( w -- ) Display
                                         an integer in free
                                         format, preceded
                                         by a space.
DD        BASE,AT,DOLIT,10,XORR          decimal?
DD        QBRAN,DOT1
DD        UDOT,EXITT                     No, display
                                         unsigned
                                         number
DOT1:
DD        STRR,SPACE,TYPES,EXITT         Yes, display
                                         signed number
```

? displays signed integer stored in memory a on the top of the parameter stack, in free format followed by a space.

```
$COLON    1,'?',QUEST    ? ( a -- ) Display the contents in a
                         memory cell.
DD        AT,DOT,EXITT
```

HEX sets numeric conversion radix in BASE to 16 for hexadecimal conversions.

$COLON	3,'HEX',HEX	HEX (--) Use radix 16 as base for numeric conversions.
DD	DOLIT,16,BASE	
DD	STORE,EXITT	

DECIMAL sets numeric conversion radix in BASE to 10 for decimal conversions.

$COLON	7,'DECIMAL',DECIM	DECIMAL (--) Use radix 10 as base for numeric conversions.
DD	DOLIT,10,BASE	
DD	STORE,EXITT	

Numeric Input

The Forth text interpreter also handles the number input to the system. It parses words out of the input stream and trtes to execute the words in sequence. When the text interpreter encounters a word which is not the name of a token in the dictionary, it then assumes that the word must be a number and attempts to convert the ASCII string to a number according to the current radix. When the text interpreter succeeds in converting the string to a number, the number is pushed on the data stack for future use if the text interpreter is in interpreting mode. If it is in compiling mode, the text interpreter will compile the number to code dictionary as an integer literal so that when the token under construction is later executed, this literal integer will be pushed on the data stack.

If the text interpreter fails to convert the word to a number, this is an error condition which will cause the text interpreter to abort, posting an error message to you, and then wait for your next line of commands.

The following figure show how a number string 123456 parsed out of the input buffer is converted to a number and pushed on the parameter stack:

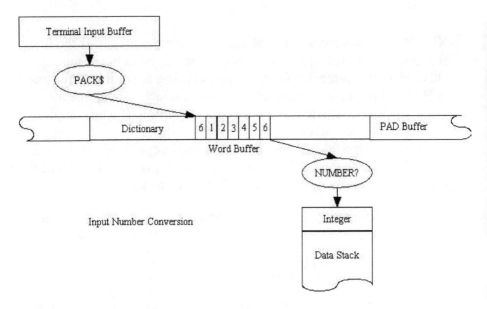

Input Number Conversion

Only two words are needed in eForth to handle input of single precision integer numbers.

DIGIT? converts a digit to its numeric value according to the current base, and NUMBER? converts a number string to a single integer.

	$COLON	6,'digit?',DIGTQ	**DIGIT? (c base -- u t) Convert a character to its numeric value. A flag indicates success.**
	DD	TOR,DOLIT,'0',SUBBB	**save radix, convert ASCII to digit**
	DD	DOLIT,9,OVER,LESS	**is digit greater than 9?**
	DD	QBRAN,DGTQ1	
	DD	DOLIT,7,SUBBB	**Yes. Convert hex to decimal digit**
	DD	DUPP,DOLIT,10,LESS,ORR	**If digit<10, change it to -1**
DGTQ1:	DD	DUPP,RFROM,ULESS	**If digit >= base, return a false flag**
	DD	EXITT	

NUMBER? converts a string of digits to a single integer. If the first character is a $ sign, the number is assumed to be in hexadecimal. Otherwise, the number will be converted using the radix value stored in BASE. For negative numbers, the first character should be a - sign. No other characters are allowed in the string. If a non-digit character is encountered, the address of the string and a false flag are returned. Successful conversion returns the integer value and a true flag. If the number is larger than 2**n, where n is the bit width of the single integer, only the modulus to 2**n will be kept.

	$COLON	7,'number?',NUMBQ	number? (a -- n T | a F) Convert a number string to integer. Push a flag on tos.
	DD	BASE,AT,TOR	save the current radix in BASE
	DD	DOLIT,0,OVER,COUNT	a 0 a+1 n --, get length of the string
	DD	OVER,CAT	get first digit
	DD	DOLIT,'$',EQUAL	is it a $ for hexadecimal base?
	DD	QBRAN,NUMQ1	
	DD	HEX,SWAP,ONEP	Yes, use hexadecimal base and adjust string
	DD	SWAP,ONEM	a 0 a+2 n-1 --
NUMQ1:	DD	OVER,CAT	get next digit
	DD	DOLIT,'-',EQUAL,TOR	Is it a - sign? Save flag.
	DD	SWAP,RAT,SUBBB,SWAP	a 0 b' n' --, adjust address b
	DD	RAT,PLUS,QDUP	a 0 b" n" n" --, adjust count n"
	DD	QBRAN,NUMQ6	
	DD	ONEM,TOR	valid count, convert string
NUMQ2:	DD	DUPP,TOR,CAT	save address b and get next digit
	DD	BASE,AT,DIGTQ	convert it according to current radix
	DD	QBRAN,NUMQ4	If it is a valid digit
	DD	SWAP,BASE,AT,STAR	multiply it by radix
	DD	PLUS,RFROM,ONEP	add to sum. Increment address b
	DD	DONXT,NUMQ2	loop back to convert the next digit

	DD	RAT,SWAP,DROP	completely convert the string. get sign
	DD	QBRAN,NUMQ3	
	DD	NEGAT	negate the sum if -flag is true
NUMQ3:	DD	SWAP	sum a --
	DD	BRAN,NUMQ5	
NUMQ4:	DD	RFROM,RFROM,DDROP	If a non-digit was encountered
	DD	DDROP,DOLIT,0	a 0 --, conversion failed
NUMQ5:	DD	DUPP	sum a a --, if success; else a 0 0 --
NUMQ6:	DD	RFROM,DDROP	discard garbage
	DD	RFROM,BASE,STORE	restore BASE
	DD	EXITT	

Derived I/O Words

All I/O words are derived from ?KEY, KEY and EMIT. The
following set defined in
eForth is particularly useful in normal programming:

NUF? returns a false flag if no character is pending in the input
buffer. After receiving a character, pause and wait for another
character. If this character is CR, return a true flag; otherwise, return
false. This word is very useful in user interruptable routines.

	$COLON	4,'nuf?',NUFQ	NUF? (-- t) Return false if no input, else pause and if CR return true.
	DD	QKEY,DUPP	got a key?
	DD	QBRAN,NUFQ1	No. return a false flag
	DD	DDROP,KEY	Yes. Get key
	DD	DOLIT,CRR,EQUAL	Is it a CR? Return a flag.
NUFQ1:	DD	EXITT	

SPACE outputs a blank space character.

```
$COLON    5,'SPACE',SPACE        SPACE ( -- ) Send the blank
                                 character to the output device.
DD        BLANK,EMIT,EXITT       send space
```

SPACES output n blank space characters.

```
          $COLON    6,'SPACES',SPACS      SPACES ( +n -- ) Send
                                          n spaces to the output
                                          device.
          DD        DOLIT,0,MAX,TOR       avoid negative numbers
          DD        BRAN,CHAR2
CHAR1:    DD        SPACE                 send one space
CHAR2:    DD        DONXT,CHAR1           loop back
          DD        EXITT
```

TYPE outputs n characters from a string in memory.

```
          $COLON    4,'TYPE',TYPES        TYPE ( b u -- )
                                          Output u characters
                                          from b.
          DD        TOR
          DD        BRAN,TYPE2            skip one loop
TYPE1:    DD        DUPP,CAT,TCHAR,EMIT   emit only printable
                                          characters
          DD        ONEP                  b+1
TYPE2:    DD        DONXT,TYPE1
          DD        DROP,EXITT            discard b
```

CR outputs a carriage-return and a line-feed.

```
$COLON    2,'CR',CR               CR ( -- ) Output a carriage
                                  return and a line feed.
DD        DOLIT,CRR,EMIT          CR
DD        DOLIT,LF,EMIT,EXITT     LF
```

String Literal Words

We've discussed integer literals and address literals, which are data structures in a colon word. Normally, a colon word has a token list in its parameter field. Tokens are 4-byte code field addresses, which are sequenced through by an address interpreter. An integer literal starts with DOLIT and is followed by a 4-byte value, which is pushed on data stack by the address interpreter. An address literal begins with a token like BRANCH, ?BRABCH and DONXT, followed by a 4-byte address to allow the address interpreter to jump to another location in the token list.

String literals are also data structures compiled in colon words, in-line with tokens. A string literal must start with a string token with a following variable length counted string. The string token knows how to handle the following string at the run time. In eForth, there are three types of string literals:

```
: XXX ... " A compiled string" ... ;
: YYY ... ." An output string" ... ;
: ZZZ ... ABORT" A warning mssage" ...;
```

In XXX, " is an immediate word which compiles the following string as a string literal preceded by a special token $"|. When $"| is executed at run time, it returns the address of this string on data stack to be used by other Forth words. In YYY, ." compiles a string literal preceded by another token ."|, which displays the compiled string at run time. ABORT" is used to compile an error message, preceded by a token abort"|. The token abort"| displays the following message and then jumps to ABORT to reset eForth system, if top of stack has a true flag. It is the error handler of eForth.

Both $"| and ."| use the word DO$, which retrieve the address of a string stored as the second item on the return stack. DO$ is a bit difficult to understand, because the starting address of the following string is the second item on the return stack. This address is pushed on the data stack so that the string can be accessed. This address must be changed so that the address interpreter will return to the token right after the compiled string. This address will allow the

address interpreter to skip over the string literal and continue to
execute the token list as intended.

```
$COLON   COMPO+3,'do$',DOSTR    do$ ( -- a ) Return the address of a
                                 compiled string.
DD       RFROM                   1st return address must be saved
DD       RAT,RFROM               2nd return address points to
                                 counted string a
DD       COUNT,PLUS              address of next token after string
                                 literal
DD       TOR,SWAP                replace 2nd return address
DD       TOR,EXITT               restore saved 1st return address
```

$"| push the address of the following string on stack. Other words
can use this address to access data stored in this string. The string is
a counted string. Its first byte is a byte count.

```
$COLON   COMPO+3,'$"|',STRQP     $"| ( -- a ) Run time routine
                                 compiled by $". Return address
                                 of a compiled string.
DD       DOSTR,EXITT             force a call to do$
```

"| displays the following string on stack. This ia a very convenient
way to send helping messages to you at run time.

```
$COLON   COMPO+3,'."|',DOTQP     ."| ( -- ) Run time routine of ." .
                                 Output a compiled string.
DD       DOSTR,COUNT,TYPES       display following string
DD       EXITT
```

Parsing

Parsing is always thought of as a very advanced topic in computer
sciences. However, because Forth uses very simple syntax rules,
parsing is easy. Forth source code consists of words, which are
ASCII strings separated by spaces and other white space characters
like tabs, carriage returns, and line feeds. The text interpreter scans
the source code, isolates words and interprets them in sequence.

After a word is parsed out of the input text stream, the text interpreter will 'interpret' it--execute it if it is a token, compile it if the text interpreter is in the compiling mode, and convert it to a number if the word is not a Forth token.

PARSE scans the source string in the terminal input buffer from where >IN points to till the end of the buffer, for a word delimited by character c. It returns the address and length of the word parsed out. PARSE calls (PARSE) to do the dirty work.

(PARSE) (b1 u1 c --b2 u2 n) From the source string starting at b1 and of u1 characters long, parse out the first word delimited by character c. Return the address b2 and length u2 of the word just parsed out and the difference n between b1 and b2. Leading delimiters are skipped over. (PARSE) is used by PARSE.

	$COLON	7,'(parse)',PARS	(PARSE) (b u c -- b u delta ; <string>) Scan string delimited by c. Return found string and its offset.
	DD	TEMP,STORE,OVER	b u b --, save c
	DD	TOR,DUPP	b u u --, save b, test u
	DD	QBRAN,PARS8	if u=0, exit
	DD	ONEM,TEMP,AT	u not 0, c=blank?
	DD	BLANK,EQUAL	
	DD	QBRAN,PARS3	u not blank, go forward
	DD	TOR	loop u times to skip blanks
PARS1:	DD	BLANK,OVER,CAT	skip leading blanks
	DD	SUBBB,ZLESS,INVER	
	DD	QBRAN,PARS2	found non-blanks character, go parsing
	DD	ONEP	
	DD	DONXT,PARS1	b+1 --, end of loop
	DD	RFROM,DROP	string is blank, exit
	DD	DOLIT,0,DUPP,EXITT	b 0 0 --
PARS2:	DD	RFROM	found non-blanks character, parse
PARS3:	DD	OVER,SWAP	b b u --, start parsing non-space characters
	DD	TOR	loop u times to parse a string

```
PARS4:   DD      TEMP,AT,OVER
         DD      CAT,SUBBB              scan for delimiter
         DD      TEMP,AT,BLANK,EQUAL
         DD      QBRAN,PARS5            c is not blank
         DD      ZLESS
PARS5:   DD      QBRAN,PARS6            c is blank, exit this
                                       loop
         DD      ONEP                  b+1 --
         DD      DONXT,PARS4           loop back to test next
                                       character
         DD      DUPP,TOR              save a copy of b at
                                       the end of the loop
         DD      BRAN,PARS7            found a valid string
PARS6:   DD      RFROM,DROP,DUPP       discard loop count
         DD      ONEP,TOR              save a copy of b+1
PARS7:   DD      OVER,SUBBB            length of the parsed
                                       string
         DD      RFROM,RFROM,SUBBB     and its offset in the
                                       buffer
         DD      EXITT                 b u 0--
PARS8:   DD      OVER,RFROM,SUBBB      b u delta --
         DD      EXITT
```

PARSE is used to implement many specialized parsing words to handle different source code. These words, including (, \, CHAR, WORD, and TOKEN are discussed in the next section.

```
$COLON   5,'parse',PARSE        PARSE ( c -- b u ; <string> )
                                Scan input stream and return
                                counted string delimited by c.
DD       TOR,TIB,INN,AT,PLUS    current input buffer pointer to
                                start parsing
DD       NTIB,AT,INN,AT,SUBBB   length of remaining string in
                                TIB
DD       RFROM,PARS             parse desired string
DD       INN,PSTOR,EXITT        move pointer to end of string
```

Parsing Words

Here is a set of words using the parser discussed earlier. They scan the following text stream for text delimited by specific terminating character, and then use the text for specific purposes. The simplest use is to insert comments inside body of source code. The most important use is to find tokens for interpreting and compiling.

.(types the following string till the next). It is used to output text to the terminal.

```
$COLON    IMEDD+2,'.(',DOTPR        .( ( -- ) Output following
                                     string up to next ).
DD        DOLIT,')',PARSE,TYPES      parse till ) and display
                                     parsed string
DD        EXITT
```

(ignores the following string till the next). It is used to place comments in source text.

```
$COLON    IMEDD+1,'(',PAREN          ( ( -- ) Ignore following
                                     string up to next ). A
                                     comment.
DD        DOLIT,')',PARSE,DDROP      parse till ) and discard
                                     parsed string
DD        EXITT
```

\ ignores all characters till end of input buffer. It is used to insert comment lines in text.

```
$COLON    IMEDD+1,'\',BKSLA          \ ( -- ) Ignore following text till the
                                     end of line.
DD        NTIB,AT,INN,STORE          make >IN equal to #TIB and
                                     terminate parsing
DD        EXITT
```

WORD parses out the next word delimited by the ASCII character c. Copy the word to the top of the code dictionary and return the address of this counted string.

$COLON	4, 'WORD', WORDD	**WORD (c -- a ; \<string>) Parse a word from input stream and copy it to code dictionary.**
DD	PARSE	**parse till c**
DD	HERE, CELLP	
DD	PACKS, EXITT	**pack parsed string to HERE buffer**

TOKEN parses the next word from the input buffer and copy the counted string to the top of the name dictionary. Return the address of this counted string.

$COLON	5, 'token', TOKEN	**TOKEN (-- a ; \<string>) Parse a word from input stream and copy it to name dictionary.**
DD	BLANK, WORDD	**parse next string delimited by spaces**
DD	EXITT	**pack parsed string to HERE buffer**

Dictionary Search

In eForth, word records are linked into a dictionary which can be searched to find valid words. A header contains four fields: a link field holding the name field address of the previous header, a name field holding the name as a counted string, a code field holding execution address of the word, and a parameter field holding data to be processed. The dictionary is a list linked through the link fields and the name fields. The basic searching function is performed by the word FIND. FIND scans the linked list to find a name which matches an input text string, and returns the code field address and the name field address of an executable token, if a match is found.

FIND is a big word, and is fairly complicated. The following flowchart, hopefully, will give you a good bird eye view of the logic involved in searching the dictionary to find a word.

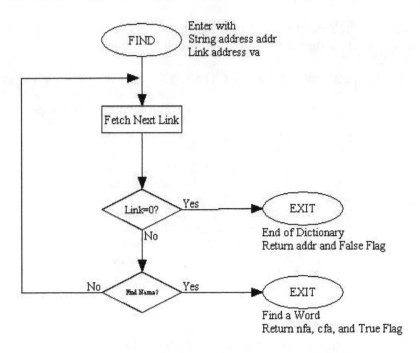

A system variable CONTEXT points to the name field of the last word in the dictionary. This is where FIND begins its search.

NAME> (nfa – cfa) Return a code field address from the name field address of a word.

$COLON	5,'name>',NAMET	NAME> (nfa -- cfa) Return a code address given a name address.
DD	COUNT,DOLIT,31,ANDD	mask lexicon byte to get length
DD	PLUS,EXITT	skip over name field

SAME? (a1 a2 n – a1 a2 f) Compare n-1 bytes in strings at a1 and a2. If the strings are the same, return a 0. If string at a1 is higher than that at a2, return a positive number; otherwise, return a negative number. FIND compares the count byte and 1st character of input string and a name. If these two bytes are the same, SAME? Is called to compare the rest of two strings. It is necessary to compare byte to byte, because strings are not aligned to cell boundaries.

	$COLON	5,'same?',SAMEQ	SAME? (a1 a2 u -- a1 a2 f \ -0+) Compare u-2 bytes in two strings. Return 0 if identical.
	DD	ONEM,TOR	compare n-1 bytes
	DD	BRAN,SAME2	skip the first round
SAME1:	DD	OVER,RAT,PLUS,CAT	get source byte
	DD	OVER,RAT,PLUS,CAT	get target byte
	DD	SUBBB,QDUP	compare
	DD	QBRAN,SAME2	same?
	DD	RFROM,DROP,EXITT	not same, f<>0
SAME2:	DD	DONXT,SAME1	same, loop for next byte
	DD	DOLIT,0,EXITT	same, f=0

FIND (a va --cfa nfa, a F) Search the dictionary for a word. A counted string at a is the name of a token to be looked up in the dictionary. The last name field address of the dictionary is stored in location va. If the string is found, both the code field address and the name field address are returned. If the string is not the name a token, the string address and a false flag are returned.

To locate a word, FIND follows the linked list and compare the names of defined tokens to the string to be searched. If the string matches the name of a token in the dictionary, code field address and a name field address are returned. If the string is not a defined token, the search will lead to a null name field. In this case, the search will be terminated and a false flag returned. The false flag thus indicates that the name searched is not a valid word.

FIND runs through the dictionary very quickly because it first compares the length and the first character in the name as a 16-bit integer. In most cases of mismatch, this comparison would fail and the next name can be reached through the link field. If the first two characters match, then SAME? is invoked to compare the rest of the name field, one byte at a time.

	$COLON	4,'find',FIND	FIND (a va -- cfa nfa | a F) Search a dictionary for a string. Return cfa and nfa if succeeded.
	DD	SWAP,DUPP,CAT	va a count --
	DD	TEMP,STORE	count saved in tmp
	DD	DUPP,AT,TOR	
	DD	TWOP,SWAP	a+2 va --, first 4 bytes saved on RS
FIND1:	DD	AT,DUPP	a+2 nfa nfa --, end of dictionary?
	DD	QBRAN,FIND6	end, return a 0
	DD	DUPP,TWOP,SWAP	a+2 nfa+2 nfa --
	DD	AT,RAT,XORR	
	DD	DOLIT,MASKK,AND D	a+2 nfa+2 f --, compare first 2 bytes
	DD	QBRAN,FIND2	2 bytes same, do SAME?
	DD	DOLIT,-1	a+2 nfa+2 -1 --, not same, repeat
	DD	BRAN,FIND3	
FIND2:	DD	TEMP,AT,SAMEQ	a+2 nfa+2 f --, compare rest of name
FIND3:	DD	QBRAN,FIND5	a+2 nfa+2 --
	DD	CELLM,TWOM	a+2 lfa --, not this name
	DD	BRAN,FIND1	go to next name
FIND5:	DD	RFROM,DROP,SWAP ,DROP	nfa+2 --
	DD	TWOM	nfa --
	DD	DUPP,NAMET,SWAP ,EXITT	cfa nfa --, find name
FIND6:	DD	RFROM,DROP	a+2 0 --, end of dictionary
	DD	SWAP,TWOM,SWAP, EXITT	a 0 --, return with 0 flag

NAME? (a -- cfa nfa, a F) Search dictionary starting at where CONTEXT points to. Name to be searched is a. Return cfa and nfa if a matching word is found. Otherwise, return the string address a and a false flag.

$COLON	5,'name?',NAMEQ	NAME? (a -- cfa nfa | a F) Search dictionary for a string.	
DD	CNTXT,FIND,EXITT	initial nfa is in CONTEXT	

Text Input

The text interpreter interprets input text stream stored in the terminal
input buffer. None of us can type perfectly. We have to allow
mistyped characters and give us opportunities to back up and correct
mistakes. To allow some minimal editing, we need three special
words to deal with backspaces and carriage return thus received: ^H,
TAP and KTAP. These words are hard to understand because they
manipulate three addresses on data stack: bot is bottom of terminal
buffer, eot is end of terminal buffer, and cur is current character
pointer.

^H (bot eot cur -- bot eot cur) Process the back-space character.
Erase the last character and decrement cur. If cur=bot, do nothing
because you cannot backup beyond the beginning of the input buffer.

	$COLON	2,'^h',BKSP	^H (bot eot cur -- bot eot cur) Backup the cursor by one character.
	DD	TOR,OVER,RFROM	bot eot bot cur --
	DD	SWAP,OVER,XORR	bot=cur?
	DD	QBRAN,BACK1	
	DD	DOLIT,BKSPP,EMIT	back space
	DD	ONEM, BLANK,EMIT	send blank
	DD	DOLIT,BKSPP,EMIT	back space again
BACK1:	DD	EXITT	bot=cur, do not back space

TAP (bot eot cur c -- bot eot cur) Echo c to output device, store c in
cur, and bump cur.

$COLON	3,'tap',TAP	TAP (bot eot cur c -- bot eot cur) Accept and echo the key stroke and bump the cursor.
DD	DUPP,EMIT	duplicate character and emit it
DD	OVER,CSTOR,ONEP	store c at cur, and increment cur
DD	EXITT	

kTAP (bot eot cur c -- bot eot cur) Process a character c in input buffer. bot is the starting address of the input buffer. eot is the end of the input buffer. cur is the current character pointer. Character c is normally stored into cur, which is increment by 1. In this case, cur is the same as eot. If c is a carriage-return, echo a space and make eot=cur. If c is a back-space, erase the last character and decrement cur.

	$COLON	4,'ktap',KTAP	**kTAP (bot eot cur -- bot eot cur) Process a key stroke, CR or backspace.**
	DD	DUPP,DOLIT,CRR,XORR	is key a return?
	DD	QBRAN,KTAP2	
	DD	DOLIT,BKSPP,XORR	is key a backspace?
	DD	QBRAN,KTAP1	
	DD	BLANK,TAP,EXITT	non of above, replace by a space
KTAP1:	DD	BKSP,EXITT	process back space
KTAP2:	DD	DROP,SWAP,DROP,DUPP	process carriage return
	DD	EXITT	

ACCEPT (b u1 --b u2) Accept u1 characters to b. u2 returned is the actual number of characters received.

	$COLON	6,'accept',ACCEP	accept (b u1 -- b u2) Accept characters to input buffer. Return with actual count.
	DD	OVER,PLUS,OVER	b b+u1 b --
ACCP1:	DD	DDUP,XORR	b+u1 = current pointer?
	DD	QBRAN,ACCP4	Yes, exit
	DD	KEY,DUPP	No, get next character
	DD	BLANK,DOLIT,127,WITHI	a valid character?
	DD	QBRAN,ACCP2	
	DD	TAP	Yes, accept it to input buffer

```
         DD        BRAN,ACCP3
ACCP2:   DD        KTAP                      No, process
                                             control character
ACCP3:   DD        BRAN,ACCP1                loop for next
                                             character
ACCP4:   DD        DROP,OVER,SUBBB           done, return
                                             actual string
                                             length

         DD        EXITT
```

QUERY is the word which accepts text input, up to 80 characters, from an input device and copies the text characters to the terminal input buffer. It also prepares the terminal input buffer for parsing by setting #TIB to the received character count and clearing >IN.

```
$COLON   5,'query',QUERY          QUERY ( -- ) Accept input
                                  stream to terminal input
                                  buffer.
DD       TIB,DOLIT,80,ACCEP       accept up to 80 character to
                                  TIB
DD       NTIB,STORE,DROP          store actual string length in
                                  #TIB
DD       DOLIT,0,INN,STORE        init >IN
DD       EXITT
```

Error Handling

In 86eForth v1.0, there was a very sophisticated error handling mechanism with CATCH and THROW. Over the years, I have never had a opportunity to make use of it. Therefore, it is taken out in 86eForth v5.2. Whenever an error occurs, the system returns to ABORT.

ABORT reset data stack and fall into the text interpreter loop QUIT.

```
$COLON   5,'ABORT',ABORT     ABORT ( -- ) Reset data stack and
                             jump to QUIT.
DD       PRESE,DOTS,QUIT     dump stack as well
```

abort"| (f --) A runtime string command compiled in front of a string of error message. If flag f is true, display the following string and jump to ABORT. If flag f is false, ignore the following string and continue executing tokens after the error message.

$COLON	COMPO+7,'abort"|',ABORQ	abort"| (f --) Run time routine of ABORT". Abort with a message.
	DD	QBRAN,ABOR2	test flag
	DD	DOSTR	get string address
ABOR1:	DD	SPACE,COUNT,TYPES	display error string
	DD	DOLIT,'?',EMIT,CR,ABORT	go pass error string
ABOR2:	DD	DOSTR,DROP,EXITT	drop error string

?STACK (--) Check data stack. If data stack underflows, display and error message and ABORT; otherwise continue executing next token.

$COLON	6,'?stack',QSTAC	?STACK (--) Abort if the data stack underflows.
DD	DEPTH,ZLESS	check only for underflow
DD	ABORQ	abort if true
DB	11,' underflow '	
DD	EXITT	

Text Interpreter Loop

Text interpreter is the heart of Forth. It is like the operating system of a computer. It is the primary interface between you and a computer. Since Forth uses very simple syntax rules--words are separated by spaces, the text interpreter is also very simple. It accepts a line of text you type on a terminal keyboard, parses out a word delimited by spaces, searches the token of this word in the dictionary and then executes it. The process is repeated until the line of text is exhausted. Then the text interpreter waits for another line of text and interprets it again. This cycle repeats until you are exhausted and turns off the computer.

In eForth, the text interpreter is encoded in the word QUIT. QUIT contains an infinite loop which repeats the QUERY and EVAL commands. QUERY accepts a line of text from the terminal and copies the text into the Terminal Input Buffer (TIB). EVAL interprets the text one word at a time till end of the line.

One of the unique features in eForth is its error handling mechanism. While EVAL is interpreting a line of text, it could encounter many error conditions: a word is not found in the dictionary and it is not a number, a compile-only word is accidentally executed interpretively, and the interpretive process may be interrupted by the words ABORT or ABORT". Wherever the error occurs, the text interpreter resets and starts over at ABORT.

$INTERPRET executes a word whose string address is on the stack. If the string is not a word, convert it to a number. If it is not a number, ABORT.

	$COLON	10,'$interpret',INTER	$INTERPRET (a --) Interpret a word. If failed, try to convert it to an integer.
	DD	NAMEQ,QDUP	word defined?
	DD	QBRAN,INTE1	No. go convert to number
	DD	AT,DOLIT,COMPO,ANDD	test compile-only lexicon bit
	DD	ABORQ	If it is compile-only, abort
	DB	13,' compile only'	
	DD	EXECU,EXITT	otherwise, execute defined word
INTE1:	DD	NUMBQ	convert to a number
	DD	QBRAN,ABOR1	not a number, abort
	DD	EXITT	

Here are some of the words used by the text interpreter.

[activates the text interpreter by storing the execution address of
$INTERPRET into the variable 'EVAL, which is executed in EVAL
while the text interpreter is in the interpretive mode.

```
$COLON   IMEDD+1,'[',LBRAC   [ ( -- ) Start the text interpreter.
DD       DOLIT,INTER         get address of $INTERPRET
DD       TEVAL,STORE,EXITT   store it in 'EVAL
```

.OK used to be a word which displays the familiar 'ok' prompt after
executing to the end of a line. In 86eForth v5.2, it displays the top 4
elements on data stack so you can see what is happening on the
stack. It is more informative than the plain 'ok', which only give you
a warm and fuzzy feeling about the system. When text interpreter is
in compiling mode, the display is suppressed.

```
        $COLON   3,'.ok',DOTOK     .OK ( -- ) Display the data
                                   stack only while
                                   interpreting.
        DD       CR,DOLIT,INTER    'EVAL contains
                                   $INTRPRET?
        DD       TEVAL,AT,EQUAL
        DD       QBRAN,DOTO1       no, exit
        DD       DOTS              yes, dump stack
DOTO1:  DD       EXITT
```

EVAL has a loop which parses tokens from the input stream and
invokes whatever is in 'EVAL to process that token, either execute it
with $INTERPRET or compile it with $COMPILE. It exits the loop
when the input stream is exhausted.

```
        $COLON   4,'eval',EVAL       EVAL ( -- ) Interpret the
                                     input stream.
EVAL1:  DD       TOKEN,DUPP,CAT      input stream empty?
        DD       QBRAN,EVAL2         yes, exit
        DD       TEVAL,ATEXE,QSTAC   no, evaluate input, check
                                     stack
        DD       BRAN,EVAL1          loop back for next word
EVAL2:  DD       DROP,DOTOK,EXITT    done, display prompt
```

PRESET initialized the data stack by copying the address in _SPP
into the data stack pointer SP (ESP).

```
$COLON   6,'preset',PRESE       PRESET ( -- ) Reset data stack
                                pointer.
DD       DOLIT,_SPP,AT,SPSTO    init data stack pointer
DD       EXITT
```

QUIT is the operating system, or a shell, of the eForth system. It is
an infinite loop eForth will not leave. It uses QUERY to accept a line
of text from the terminal and then let EVAL parse out the tokens and
execute them. After a line is processed, it displays the top of data
stack and wait for the next line of text. When an error occurred
during execution, it displays the command which caused the error
with an error message. After the error is reported, it re-initializes the
system by jumping to ABORT.

Because the behavior of EVAL can be changed by storing either
$INTERPRET or $COMPILE into 'EVAL, QUIT exhibits the dual
nature of a text interpreter and a compiler.

```
        $COLON   4,'quit',QUIT          QUIT ( -- ) Reset
                                        return stack pointer
                                        and start text
                                        interpreter.
        DD       DOLIT,_RPP,AT,RPSTO    init return stack
                                        pointer
QUIT1:  DD       LBRAC                  start interpretation
QUIT2:  DD       QUERY                  get input
        DD       EVAL                   process input
        DD       BRAN,QUIT2             continue till error
```

Chapter 9. - Colon Compiler

After wading through the text interpreter, the Forth compiler will be an easy piece of cake, because the compiler uses almost all the modules used by the text interpreter. What the compile does, over and above the text interpreter, is to build various structures required by the new words you add to the .data segment. Here is a list of these structures:

- Colon words

- Constants

- Variables

- Integer literals

- String literals

- Address literals and control structures

A special concept of immediate words is difficult to grasp at first. It is required in the compiler because of the needs in building different data and control structures in a colon word. To understand the Forth compiler fully, you have to be able to differential and relate the actions taken during compile time and actions taken during run time. Once these concepts are clear, the whole Forth system will become transparent.

This set stage for enlightenment to strike.

Interpreter and Compiler

The Forth compiler is the twin brother of the Forth text interpreter. They share many common properties and use lots of common code. In eForth, the implementation of the compiler clearly reflects this special duality. Two interesting words [and] causes the text interpreter to switch back and forth between the compiler mode and interpreter mode.

Since 'EVAL @EXECUTE is used in EVAL to process a token parsed out of a line of text, the contents in 'EVAL determines the behavior of the text interpreter. If $INTERPRET is stored in 'EVAL, as [does, tokens are executed or interpreted. If we invoke] to store $COMPILE into 'EVAL, the token will not be executed, but compiled to the top of dictionary. This is exactly the behavior desired by the colon word compiler in building a list of tokens in the parameter field of a new colon word in dictionary.

$COMPILE normally adds a token to the dictionary. However, there are two exceptions it must handle. If a string parsed out of the input stream is not a word in the dictionary, the string will be converted to a number. If the string can be converted to an integer, the integer is then compiled into the dictionary as an integer literal, which consists of a special token DOLIT followed by the integer. The other exception is that a token found in the dictionary could be an immediate word, which must be executed immediately, not compiled to the dictionary. Immediate words are used to compile structures in colon words.

' (tick) searches the next word in the input stream for a token in the dictionary. It returns the code field address of the token if successful. Otherwise, it displays an error message.

```
$COLON     1,"'",TICK     ' ( -- cfa ) Search dictionary for the next
                          word in input stream.
DD         TOKEN,NAMEQ    word defined?
DD         QBRAN,ABOR1
DD         EXITT          yes, push code field address
```

ALLOT allocates n bytes of memory on the top of the dictionary. Once allocated, the compiler will not touch the memory locations. It is possible to allocate and initialize this array using the command ',' .

```
$COLON   5,'ALLOT',ALLOT        ALLOT ( n -- ) Allocate n bytes
                                to the code dictionary.
DD       CP,PSTOR,EXITT         adjust dictionary pointer
```

, (comma) adds the execution address of a token on the top of the data stack to the code dictionary, and thus compiles a token to the growing token list of the word currently under construction.

```
$COLON   1,',',COMMA                    , ( w -- ) Compile
                                        an integer into the
                                        code dictionary.
DD       HERE,DUPP,CELLP,CP,STORE,      advance CP
DD       STORE,EXITT                    compile w to
                                        dictionary
```

COMPILE is used in a colon word. It causes the next token after COMPILE to be added to the top of the code dictionary. It therefore forces the compilation of a token at the run time.

```
$COLON   COMPO+7,'compile',COMPI    COMPILE ( - )
                                    Compile the next
                                    address in colon list
                                    to code dictionary.
DD       RFROM,DUPP,AT,COMMA        compile address
DD       CELLP,TOR,EXITT            adjust return
                                    address
```

[COMPILE] acts similarly, except that it compiles the next word immediately. It causes the following word to be compiled, even if the following word is usually an immediate word which would otherwise be executed.

```
$COLON   IMEDD+9,'[compile]',BCOMP   [COMPILE] ( -- ; <string>
                                     ) Compile the next
                                     immediate word into code
                                     dictionary.
DD       TICK,COMMA,EXITT            search next word and
                                     compile its cfa
```

LITERAL compiles an integer literal to the current colon word under construction. The integer literal is taken from the data stack, and is preceded by the token doLIT. When this colon word is executed, doLIT will extract the integer from the token list and push it back on the data stack. LITERAL compiles an address literal if the compiled integer happens to be an execution address of a token. The address will be pushed on the data stack at the run time by doLIT.

$COLON	IMEDD+7,'literal',LITER	LITERAL (w –) Compile tos to dictionary as an integer literal.
DD	COMPI,DOLIT,COMMA	compile DOLIT and w as an integer literal
DD	EXITT	this is a integer literal in a colon word

$," compiles a string literal. The string is taken from the input stream and is terminated by the double quote character. $," only copies the counted string to the code dictionary. A token which makes use of the counted string at run time must be compiled before the string. It is used by ." and $".

$COLON	3,'$,"',STRCQ	$," (–) Compile a literal string up to next " .
DD	DOLIT,'"',PARSE,HERE,	compile string to code dictionary
DD	PACKS COUNT,PLUS	calculate aligned end of string
DD	CP,STORE,EXITT	adjust the code pointer

Control Structures

A set of immediate words are defined in eForth to build control structures in colon words. The control structures used in eForth are the following:

Conditional	`IF ... THEN`
branch	
	`IF ... ELSE ... THEN`
Finite loop	`FOR ... NEXT`
	`FOR ... AFT ... THEN... NEXT`
Infinite loop	`BEGIN ... AGAIN`
Indefinite loop	`BEGIN ... UNTIL`
	`BEGIN ... WHILE ... REPEAT`

This set of words is more powerful than the ones in figForth model because they do not do error checking and thus permit multiple entries into and exits from a control structure. However, it is not recommended that you overlap the control structures. In the learning stage of Forth language, it will do you good to remember that:

Control structures can be nested, but not overlapped.

A control structure contains one or more address literals, which causes execution to branch out of the normal linear sequence. Control structure words are immediate words which compile address literals and resolve branch addresses.

One should note that BEGIN and THEN do not compile any code. They executes during compilation to set up and to resolve branch addresses in address literals. IF, ELSE, WHILE, UNTIL, and AGAIN do compile address literals with BRANCH and ?BRANCH tokens. To set up a counted loop, FOR compiles >R to begin the loop, and NEXT compiles a DONXT address literal to terminate the loop. There are many excellent examples using COMPILE and [COMPILE], and they are worthy of your attention.

In the stack comments of the following control structure words, I will use a lower case 'a' to indicate a pointer to the address field in an address literal. The address field is initialized to 0, and will be filled later when the target address is known. I will use a upper case 'A' to indicate a target address which will be used to fill the address field in an address literal.

FOR starts a FOR-NEXT loop structure in a colon definition. It compiles >R, which pushes a loop count on return stack. It also leaves the address of next token on data stack, so that NEXT will compile a DONXT address literal with the correct branch address.

$COLON	IMEDD+3,'FOR',FORR	FOR (-- a) Start a FOR-NEXT loop structure in a colon definition.
DD	COMPI,TOR	compile >R to start a FOR-NEXT loop
DD	HERE,EXITT	leave address a of next token

NEXT Terminate a FOR-NEXT loop structure, by compiling a DONXT address literal, branch back to the address A on data stack.

$COLON	IMEDD+4,'NEXT',NEXT	NEXT (a --) Terminate a FOR-NEXT loop structure.
DD	COMPI,DONXT,COMMA	Compile DONXT address literal with address a
DD	EXITT	

BEGIN starts an infinite or indefinite loop structure. Ir does not compile anything, but leave the current token address on data stack to resolve address literals compiled later.

| $COLON | IMEDD+5,'BEGIN',BEGIN | BEGIN (-- a) Start an infinite or indefinite loop structure. |
| DD | HERE,EXITT | leave address a of next token |

UNTIL terminate a BEGIN-UNTIL indefinite loop structure. It compiles a ?BRANCH address literal using the address on data stack.

| $COLON | IMEDD+5,'UNTIL',UNTIL | UNTIL (a --) Terminate a BEGIN-UNTIL indefinite loop structure. |
| DD | COMPI,QBRAN,COMMA | compile ?BRANCH address literal with |

```
                                           address a
DD        EXITT
```

AGAIN terminate a BEGIN-AGAIN infinite loop structure. . It compiles a BRANCH address literal using the address on data stack.

$COLON	IMEDD+5,'AGAIN',AGAIN	**AGAIN (a --) Terminate a BEGIN-AGAIN infinite loop structure.**
DD	COMPI,BRAN,COMMA	**compile BRANCH address literal with address a**
DD	EXITT	

IF starts a conditional branch structure. It compiles a ?BRANCH address literal, with a 0 in the address field. It leaves the address of this address field on data stack. This address will later be resolved by ELSE or THEN in closing the true clause in the branch structure.

$COLON	IMEDD+2,'IF',IFF	**IF (-- A) Begin a conditional branch structure.**
DD	COMPI,QBRAN,HERE	**compile ?BRANCH address literal, leave address A**
DD	DOLIT,0,COMMA,EXITT	**init address field to 0**

AHEAD starts a forward branch structure. It compiles a BRANCH address literal, with a 0 in the address field. It leaves the address of this address field on data stack. This address will later be resolved when the branch structure is closed.

$COLON	IMEDD+5,'ahead',AHEAD	**AHEAD (-- A) Compile a forward branch instruction.**
DD	COMPI,BRAN,HERE	**compile BRANCH address literal, leave address A**
DD	DOLIT,0,COMMA,EXITT	**init address field to 0**

REPEAT terminates a BEGIN-WHILE-REPEAT indefinite loop structure. . It compiles a BRANCH address literal with address a left by BEGIN, and use the address of next token to resolve the address literal at A.

$COLON	IMEDD+6,'REPEAT',REPEA	**REPEAT (A a --)** **Terminate a BEGIN-** **WHILE-REPEAT** **indefinite loop.**
DD	AGAIN,HERE,SWAP,STORE	**compile BRANCH** **address literal with** **address a**
DD	EXITT	**resolve address at A with** **current token address**

THEN terminates a conditional branch structure. It uses the address of next token to resolve the address literal at A left by IF or ELSE.

$COLON	IMEDD+4,'THEN',THENN	**THEN (A --) Terminate a** **conditional branch** **structure.**
DD	HERE,SWAP,STORE,EXITT	**resolve address at A with** **current token address**

AFT jumps to THEN in a FOR-AFT-THEN-NEXT loop the first time through. It compiles a BRANCH address literal and leaves its address field on stack. This address will be resolved by THEN. It also replaces address A left by FOR by the address of next token so that NEXT will compile a DONXT address literal to jump back here at run time.

$COLON	IMEDD+3,'AFT',AFT	**AFT (a -- a A) Jump to THEN in** **a FOR-AFT-THEN-NEXT loop** **the first time through.**
DD	DROP,AHEAD	**compile a BRANCH address** **literal and leave A**
DD	BEGIN,SWAP,EXIT	**replace a with address of current** **token**

ELSE (A--A) starts the false clause in an IF-ELSE-THEN structure. It compiles a BRANCH address literal. It uses the current token address to resolve the branch address in A, and replace A with the address of its address literal.

$COLON	IMEDD+4,'ELSE',ELSEE	ELSE (A -- A) Start the false clause in an IF-ELSE-THEN structure.
DD	AHEAD,SWAP	compile BRANCH address literal. resolve address at A
DD	THENN,EXITT	with current token address. Replace A by literal address

WHILE (a--Aa) compiles a ?BRANCH address literal in a BEGIN-WHILE-REPEAT loop. The address A of this address literal is swapped with address a left by BEGIN, so that REPEAT will resolve all loose ends and build the loop structure correctly.

| $COLON | IMEDD+5,'WHILE',WHILEE | WHILE (a -- A a) Conditional branch out of a BEGIN-WHILE-REPEAT loop. |
| DD | IFF,SWAP,EXITT | compile BRANCH address literal. Leave literal address A |

String Literals

Character strings are very important data structures for the program to communicate with you. Error messages, appropriate warnings and suggestions must be displayed to help you using the system in a friendly way. Character strings are compiled in the colon words as string literals. Each string literal consists of a string token which will use the compiled string to do things, and a counted string. The first byte in a counted string is the length of the string. Thus a string may have 0 to 255 characters in it.

ABORT" compiles an error message. This error message is display if top item on the stack is non-zero. The rest of the words in the word is skipped and eForth resets to ABORT. If top of stack is 0, ABORT" skips over the error message and continue executing the following token list.

$COLON	IMEDD+6,'ABORT"',ABRTQ	ABORT" (-- ; <string>) Conditional abort with an error message.
DD	COMPI,ABORQ,STRCQ	compile abort"| string literal with following string
DD	EXITT	

$" compiles a character string. When it is executed, only the address of the string is left on the data stack. You will use this address to access the string and individual characters in the string as a string array.

$COLON	IMEDD+2,'$"',STRQ	$" (-- ; <string>) Compile an inline string literal.
DD	COMPI,STRQP,STRCQ	compile $"| string literal with following string
DD	EXITT	

." compiles a character string which will be displayed when the word containing it is executed in the runtime. This is the best way to present messages to the user.

$COLON	IMEDD+2,'."',DOTQ	." (-- ; <string>) Compile an inline string literal to be typed out at run time.
DD	COMPI,DOTQP,STRCQ	compile ." string literal with following string
DD	EXITT	

Colon Word Compiler

We had discussed how the compiler compiles tokens and structures into the parameter field of a colon word in dictionary. To build a new word, we have to build an header before the parameter field. A header has a link field, a name field, a code field, and a parameter field. Here are the tools to build these fields.

?UNIQUE is used to display a warning message to show that the name of a new word already existing in dictionary. eForth does not mind your reusing the same name for different words. However, giving many words the same name is a potential cause of problems in maintaining software projects. It is to be avoided if possible and ?UNIQUE reminds you of it.

```
$COLON   7,'?unique',UNIQU   ?UNIQUE ( a -- a )
                             Display a warning
                             message if the word
                             already exists.
DD       DUPP,NAMEQ          Word defined?
DD       QBRAN,UNIQ1
DD       DOTQP               redefinitions are OK
DB       7,' reDef '         but the user should be
                             warned
DD       OVER,COUNT,TYPES    just in case it is not
                             intended
UNIQ1:  DD   DROP,EXITT
```

$,n builds a new name field in dictionary using the name already moved to the top of dictionary by PACK$. It pads the link field with the address stored in LAST. A new token can now be built in the code dictionary.

```
$COLON   3,'$,n',SNAME    $,n ( nfa -- ) Build a
                          new dictionary name
                          using the string at nfa.
DD       DUPP,CAT         null input?
DD       QBRAN,PNAM1
DD       UNIQU            redefinition?
DD       DUPP,COUNT,PLUS  skip over name field
DD       CP,STORE         CP points to code field
```

			now
	DD	DUPP,LAST,STORE	save nfa for dictionary link
	DD	CELLM	link address
	DD	CNTXT,AT,SWAP	
	DD	STORE,EXITT	fill link field with CONTEXT
PNAM1:	DD	STRQP	warning message
	DB	5,' name'	null input
	DD	BRAN,ABOR1	

$COMPILE builds the body of a new colon word. A complete colon word also requires a header in the name dictionary, and its code field must start with a CALL doLIST instruction. These extra works are performed by :. Colon words are the most prevailing type of words in eForth. In addition, eForth has a few other defining words which create other types of new words in the dictionary.

	$COLON	8,'$compile',SCOMP	**$COMPILE (a --)** **Compile next word** **to code dictionary as** **a token or literal.**
	DD	NAMEQ,QDUP	**word defined?**
	DD	QBRAN,SCOM2	
	DD	AT,DOLIT,IMEDD,ANDD	**immediate?**
	DD	QBRAN,SCOM1	
	DD	EXECU,EXITT	**its immediate, execute**
SCOM1:	DD	COMMA,EXITT	**its not immediate, compile**
SCOM2:	DD	NUMBQ	**try to convert to number**
	DD	QBRAN,ABOR1	
	DD	LITER,EXITT	**compile number as integer literal**

OVERT links a new word to the dictionary and thus makes it available for dictionary searches.

$COLON	5,'overt',OVERT	OVERT (--) Link a new word into the current dictionary.
DD	LAST,AT	
DD	CNTXT,STORE,EXITT	initialize CONTEXT from LAST

; terminates a colon word. It compiles an EXIT to the end of the token list, links this new word to the dictionary, and then reactivates the interpreter.

$COLON	IMEDD+COMPO+1,';', SEMIS	; (--) Terminate a colon definition.
DD	COMPI,EXITT	compile EXIT
DD	LBRAC,OVERT,EXITT	return to interpret mode

] turns the interpreter to a compiler.

$COLON	1,']',RBRAC	] (--) Start compiling the words in the input stream.
DD	DOLIT,SCOMP	change 'EVAL to $COMPIL
DD	TEVAL,STORE,EXITT	switch to compile mode

: creates a new header and start a new colon word. It takes the following string in the input stream to be the name of the new colon word, by building a new header with this name in the name dictionary. It then compiles a CALL doLIST instruction at the beginning of the code field in the code dictionary. Now, the code dictionary is ready to accept a token list.] is now invoked to turn the text interpreter into a compiler, which will compile the following words in the input stream to a token list in the code dictionary. The new colon word is terminated by ;, which compiles an EXIT to terminate the token list, and executes [to turn the compiler back to text interpreter.

$COL	1,':',COLON	: (-- ; <string>) Start a new colon
ON		definition using next word as its name.
DD	TOKEN,SNAME	get next string and build new name field
DD	DOLIT,DOLST,COMMA	compile DOLST into code field
DD	RBRAC,EXITT	switch to compile mode

IMMEDIATE sets the immediate lexicon bit in the name field of the new word just compiled. When the compiler encounters a word with this bit set, it will not compile this words into the token list under construction, but execute the token immediately. This bit allows structure words to build special structures in the colon words, and to process special conditions when the compiler is running.

$COLON	9,'IMMEDIATE',IMMED	IMMEDIATE (--) Make the last compiled word an immediate word.
DD	DOLIT,IMEDD	immediate bit
DD	LAST,AT,CAT,ORR	add it to lexicon byte in last name field
DD	LAST,AT,CSTOR,EXITT	Store back to lexicon byte

Defining Words

The concept of defining word is a very unique feature of Forth, in that it allows you to define new classes of words which can make specific use of data stored in their parameter fields. Each class of words share the same interpreter encoded in a routine pointed to by the address in its code field. When a word is executed by $NEXT, which is LODSD JMP [EAX], EAX points to the code field of this word, and data in the parameter field can be accessed at EAX+4 and beyond. You can design your own interpreter and create a new class of words.

In 86eForth v5.2, I provide the following defining words: , CREATE, CONSTANT and VARIABLE. CREATE and VARIABLE use the same inner interpreter DOVAR, and

CONSTANT uses DOCON. CONSTANT and VARIABLE allocate only 4 bytes for their parameter fields. CRATE, however, let you specific the size of parameter field.

CREATE creates a new array without allocating memory. Memory is allocated using ALLOT.

$COLON	6 , 'CREATE' , CREAT	**CREATE (-- ; <string>) Compile a new array entry without allocating code space.**
DD	TOKEN , SNAME , OVERT	**build new link and name fields**
DD	DOLIT , DOVAR , COMMA	**compile DOVAR into code field**
DD	EXITT	

CONSTANT creates a new constant, initialized to the value on top of stack.

$COLON	8 , 'CONSTANT' , CONST	**CONSTANT (n -- ; <string>) Compile a new constant.**
DD	TOKEN , SNAME , OVERT	**build new link and name fields**
DD	DOLIT , DOCON , COMMA	**compile DOCON into code field**
DD	COMMA , EXITT	**compile n into parameter field**

VARIABLE creates a new variable, initialized to 0.

$COLON	8 , 'VARIABLE' , VARIA	**VARIABLE (-- ; <string>) Compile a new variable initialized to 0.**
DD	CREAT , DOLIT , 0 , COMMA	**compile link, name, and DOVAR code field**
DD	EXITT	**init parameter field to 0**

Chapter 10. - Utilities

eForth is a very small system and only a very small set of tools are provided in the system. Nevertheless, this set of tools is powerful enough to help you debug new words you add to the system. They are also very interesting programming examples on how to use the words in eForth to build applications.

Generally, the tools presents the information stored in different parts of the memory in the appropriate format to let the use inspect the results as he executes words in the eForth system and words he defined himself. The tools include memory dump, stack dump, dictionary dump, and a colon word decompiler.

Memory Dump

DUMP dumps 128 bytes starting at address b to the terminal. It dumps 16 bytes to a line. A line begins with the address of the first byte, followed by 16 bytes shown in hex, 3 columns per bytes. At the end of a line are the 16 bytes shown in ASCII code. Non-printable characters by replaced by underscores.

	$COLON	4,'DUMP',DUMP	**DUMP (a --)** **Dump 128 bytes from a, in a formatted manner.**
	DD	DOLIT,7	**set line count to 7 for 8 lines**
	DD	TOR	**start count down loop**
DUMP1:	DD	CR,DUPP,DOLIT,8,UDOTR	**display address**
	DD	SPACE,DOLIT,15	**add a space**
	DD	TOR	
DUMP2:	DD	COUNT,DOLIT,3,UDOTR	**display 16 bytes of data**
	DD	DONXT,DUMP2	
	DD	SPACE,DUPP	**add space**
	DD	DOLIT,16,SUBBB	**back up 16 bytes**
	DD	DOLIT,16,TYPES	**display 16 byte of**

```
                                              text
   DD        DONXT,DUMP1                       loop till done
   DD        DROP
   DD        EXITT
```

Stack Dump

In 86eForth v1.0, .S was used to display all the elements on data stack. In 86eForth v5.2, it is used by .OK to display only the top 4 elements, and it is not necessary to have a separated tool word to dump the stack. Showing the top 4 element on the stack automatically is much informative than the simple 'OK' message.

.S displays 4 top elements on data stack. The top item is shown towards the right and followed by the characters >. .S is used by .OK after a line of text is interpreted successfully.

One important discipline in learning Forth is to learn how to use the data stack effectively. All words must consume their input parameters on the stack and leave only their intended results on the stack. Sloppy usage of the data stack is often the cause of bugs which are very difficult to detect later as unexpected items left on the stack could result in unpredictable behavior. Automatic dumping the stack by .S will be very helpful in Forth programming as you can always see what's on top of data stack.

```
$COLON  2,'.s',DOTS       .S ( ... -- ... ) Display the contents of the
                          data stack.
DD      TOR,TOR,TOR       Save 3 items on stack
DD      DUPP,DOT,RFROM    dump 4th item
DD      DUPP,DOT,RFROM    dump 3rd item
DD      DUPP,DOT,RFROM    dump 2nd item
DD      DUPP,DOT          dump 1st item
DD      DOTQP
DB      3,' > '           display separator
DD      EXITT
```

How about the return stack? While the text interpreter waits for you to type something, the return stack does not have anything of interests. When high level colon words are executing, the return stack grows and shrinks dynamically, and it is very difficult to capture and interpret rapidly transient information on return stack. Therefore, almost all Forth systems do not provide tools to examine the return stack.

In conventional programming environment, you set up break points to stop program execution, and then you can examine CPU registers, memory and stacks. Then, the return stack will show you how routines are nested and allows you to see where bugs are hiding. In Forth, words can be executed individually and naturally break at the ends. Pertinent data are most likely preserved on data stack, and that's where you can discover problems.

Dictionary Dump

The Forth dictionary contains all the words defined in the system, ready for execution and compilation. WORDS allows you to examine the dictionary and to look for the correct names of words in case you are not sure of their spellings. WORDS follows the dictionary thread in system variable CONTEXT and displays the names of each word in the dictionary. The dictionary thread can be traced easily because the link field in the header of a word points to the name field of the previous word. The link field of the next word is one cell below its name field.

Since the name fields are linked into a list in the dictionary, it is fairly easy to locate a token by searching its name. However, finding the name of a token from the execution address of the token is more difficult, because the length of name field is variable.

It is necessary to find the name field address of a token from its code field address, if we wanted to decompile a token list in the dictionary. This reversed search is accomplished by the word >NAME.

>NAME finds the name field address of a token from its code field address. If the token does not exist in the dictionary, it returns a false flag. >NAME is the mirror image of the word NAME>, which returns the code field address of a token from its name field address.

Since the code field is right after the name field, whose length is stored in the lexicon byte, NAME> is trivial. >NAME is more complicated because we have to search the dictionary to acertain the name field address.

```
          $COLON   5,'>name',TNAME          >NAME ( cfa -- nfa |
                                            F ) Convert code
                                            address to a name
                                            address.
          DD       CNTXT                    dictionary link
TNAM2:    DD       AT,DUPP                   last word in a
                                            dictionary?
          DD       QBRAN,TNAM4              Yes, reach end of
                                            dictionary
          DD       DDUP,NAMET,XORR          No, compare name
          DD       QBRAN,TNAM3             word not found
          DD       CELLM                    continue with next
                                            word
          DD       BRAN,TNAM2
TNAM3:    DD       SWAP,DROP,EXITT          found word, return
                                            nfa
TNAM4:    DD       DDROP,DOLIT,0,EXITT      end of dictionary.
                                            Return false flag
```

.ID displays the name of a token, given its name field address. It also replaces non-printable characters in a name by under-scores.

```
          $COLON   3,'.id',DOTID           .ID ( nfa -- ) Display
                                            the name at name
                                            field address.
          DD       QDUP                     if zero no name
          DD       QBRAN,DOTI1
          DD       COUNT,DOLIT,01FH,ANDD    mask lexicon bits
          DD       TYPES,EXITT              display name string
DOTI1:    DD       DOTQP                    no name
          DB       9,' {noName}'
          DD       EXITT
```

WORDS displays all the names in the dictionary. The order of words is reversed from the compiled order. The last defined word is shown first.

```
          $COLON   5,'WORDS',WORDS    WORDS ( -- ) Display the
                                      names in the context
                                      dictionary.
          DD       CR,CNTXT           start at CONTEXT
WORS1:    DD       AT,QDUP            end of dictionary?
          DD       QBRAN,WORS2        Yes, exit
          DD       DUPP,SPACE,DOTID   display a name
          DD       CELLM,NUFQ         user control
          DD       QBRAN,WORS1        repeat next word
          DD       DROP               stop by user
WORS2:    DD       EXITT
```

The Simplest Decompiler

Bill Muench and I spent much of our spare time in July, 1990 to
build and polish the eForth Model and the first implementation on
8086/MS-DOS. One evening he called me and told me about this
smallest and greatest Forth decompiler, only three lines of source
code. I was very skeptical because I knew how to build a Forth
decompiler. If a Forth colon word contains only a simple list of
execution addresses, it is a trivial task to decompile it. However,
there are many different data and control structures in a colon word.
To deal with all these structures, it is logically impossible to have a
three line decompiler.

I told Bill that I had to see it to believe. The next time we met, he
read the source code in assembly and I entered it into the eForth
model. The decompiler had 24 words and worked the first time after
we reassemble the source code.

SEE searches the dictionary for the next word in the input stream
and returns its code field address. Then it scans the list of code field
addresses (tokens) in the parameter word. If the token fetched out of
the token list matches an code field address of a word in dictionary,
the name will be displayed by the command .ID. If the token does
not match any word in the dictionary, it must be part of a data
structure and it is displayed by U. one byte at a time. This way, the
decompiler ignores all the data structures and control structures in
the colon word, and only displays valid words in the token list.

After you type in SEE <name>, hit the returns twice very quickly so that the decompiler will be stopped before spitting out too many line of text. It might be a nice computer game to see who can stop it the fastest.

	$COLON	3,'SEE',SEE	SEE (-- ; <string>) A simple decompiler. Updated for byte machines, 08mar98cht
	DD	TICK	starting address
	DD	CR,CELLP	
SEE1:	DD	ONEP,DUPP,AT,DUPP	does it contain a zero?
	DD	QBRAN,SEE2	
	DD	TNAME	is it a name?
SEE2:	DD	QDUP	name address or zero
	DD	QBRAN,SEE3	
	DD	SPACE,DOTID	display name
	DD	ONEP,TWOP	next token
	DD	BRAN,SEE4	
SEE3:	DD	DUPP,CAT,UDOT	display number
SEE4:	DD	NUFQ	user control
	DD	QBRAN,SEE1	decompile next token
	DD	DROP,EXITT	

Hardware Reset

When 86eForth v5.2 starts under Visual Studio, the machine instruction routine MAIN at the beginning of .code segment is executed. What happens next can be:

1. MAIN sets up the data stack and the return stack in the .stack segment.

2. COLD initializes system variables and sends sign-on message.

3. ABORT resets the data stack.

4. QUIT resets the return stack and enters the infinite QUERY-EVAL loop.

In 86eForth v5.2, system variables are initialized in the .data segment already, and COLD has very little to do, except sending out sign-on message and then jumping to ABORT.

ABORT is an important step, because it is where the Forth system resets when an error occurs. It is the error handler.

In an application, you generally will construct a different infinite loop which monitors a set of input devices, and drive output devices responding to the input signals. However, if your application sometimes needs human intervention, you can set up conditions that the system will invoke QUIT to enter text interpreter loop to give you back the full control over the computer. QUIT has the nice property that it does not clear the data stack, which may have important information you like to preserve.

COLD is a high level word executed upon power-up. Its most important functions are to initialize the system variables, sends out sign-on message, and then falls into the text interpreter loop through ABORT.

```
        $COLON  4,'cold',COLD        COLD ( -- ) The high
                                     level cold start
                                     sequence.
COLD1:  DD      HEX,CR,DOTQP         set base
        DB      13,'86eForth v'      sign-on message
        DB      VER+'0','.',EXT+'0'  version and extension
        DD      CR,OVERT             init data stack
        DD      ABORT                start interpretation
```

Chapter 11. - Some Final Thoughts

Congratulations if you reach this point the first time. As you can see, we have traversed a complete Forth system from the beginning to the end, and it is not as difficult as you might have thought before you began. But, think again what we have accomplished. It is a complete operating system with an integrated interpreter and an integrated compiler all together. If you look in the memory, the whole system is less than 8 Kbytes. What else can you do with 8 Kbytes these days?

Forth is like Zen. It is simple, it is accessible, and it can be understood in its entirety without devoting your whole life to it.

Is this the end? Not really. There are many topics important in Forth but we had chose to ignore in this simple model. They include multitasking, virtual memory, interrupt control, programming style, source code management, and yes, metacompilation. However, these topics can be considered advanced applications of Forth. Once the fundamental principles in Forth are understood, these topics can be subject for further investigations at your leisure.

Forth is not an end to itself. It is only a tool, as useful as you intend it to be. The most important thing is how you can use it to solve your problems and build useful applications. What eForth gives you is the understanding of this tool. It is up to you to make use of it.

Master Chef butchers an ox

I like to share two Chinese folklores with you. They were not related to Zen, but they were Zen really. One story was written by Chuang Tzu (369-286 BC）

庖丁解牛 庄子   *Master Chef butchers an ox*

庖丁為文惠君解牛，   *Master chef butchers an ox for Duke Wen Hui.*

手之所觸，	The places his hand touched,
肩之所倚，	His shoulder leaned against,
足之所履，	His foot stepped on,
膝之所踦，	His knee pressed upon,
砉然嚮然，	Came apart with a sound,
奏刀騞然，	He moved the blade, making a noise,
莫不中音：	That never fell out of rhythm.
合於《桑林》之舞，	It harmonized with the Mulberry Woods Dance,
乃中《經首》之會。	Like music from ancient times.
文惠君曰：「嘻，善哉！	Duke Wen Hui exclaimed: Ah"! Excellent!
技蓋至此乎？」	Your skill is so much advanced! "
庖丁釋刀對曰：	Master chef puts down the knife and answered:
「臣之所好者，道也，	"What I follow is Tao,
進乎技矣。	Which is beyond skills.
始臣之解牛之時，	When I started butchering,
所見無非全牛者；	I saw the whole ox.
三年之後，	After three years,
未嘗見全牛也。	I no longer saw the whole ox.
方今之時，臣以神遇，	Nowadays, I see it with my mind
而不以目視	Not with my eyes.
官知止	My senses are inactive,
而神欲行。	My mind directs the movements.
依乎天理，	It follows natural laws,
批大郤，	Separating large gaps,
導大窾，	Entering large openings,
因其固然。	Following its natural structure.
技經肯綮之未嘗，	The knife has never hesitated at tendons
而況大軱乎！	Not even the larger bones!
良庖歲更刀，	A good chef changes knife every year,
割也；	Because he cuts.

族庖月更刀，	An bad chef changes knife every month,
折也。	Because he hacks.
今臣之刀十九年矣，	I have used this knife for nineteen years.
所解數千牛矣，	It has butchered thousands of oxen,
而刀刃若新發於硎。	The blade is still like newly sharpened.
彼節者有閒，	There are spaces among joints,
而刀刃者無厚，	And the blade has no thickness.
以無厚入有閒，	Insert no thickness into spaces,
恢恢乎其於游刃	The blade swishes through,
必有餘地矣，	With plenty of room to spare!
是以十九年	That's why after nineteen years,
而刀刃若新發於硎。	The blade is still like newly sharpened.
雖然，每至於族，	Nevertheless, every time I butcher,
吾見其難為，	I see the difficulties,
怵然為戒，	I proceed with caution,
視為止，	My senses concentrate,
行為遲；	My movement slows down.
動刀甚微，	I move the knife slightly,
謋然已解，	Whump! It has already separated.
如土委地。	And falls to the ground like mud.
提刀而立，	I stand holding the knife,
為之四顧，	And look all around it.
為之躊躇滿志，	The work gives me much satisfaction.
善刀而藏之。」	I clean my knife and put it away."
文惠君曰：「善哉！	Duke Wen Hui said: "Excellent!
吾聞庖丁之言，	I listen to your words,
得養生焉。」	And learn the Tao of life."

Wow! A blade of no thickness swishes through space, with plenty of room to spare! Isn't that the tool we need to do software?

Computers keep changing, getting bigger and bigger. Software and software tools keep changing, getting bigger and bigger. Software seems to wear out like chef's knives, and you have to upgrade every year to keep up.

eForth is like master chef's knife. It is small and it is sharp. You can embed it on any computer, and then, you can use it to solve any problem. It does not wear out, and you can use it year after year.

Swordsman

The other story is actually a poem by a Tang poet name Ja Dao
(779～843 AD).

剑客　贾岛	**Swordsman by Ja Dao**
十年磨一剑，	I polish this sword for ten years.
霜刃未曾试。	The shining blade has never been tested.
今日把示君，	Today I show it to you.
谁有不平事？	Is there any injustice to avenge?

I have polished this eForth system for 26 years. I had used it to make
a living in these years, and found it extremely useful. It is in your
hand now. I wish you good luck.

Psalm 119

OK. Enough of the Eastern philosophies. Anything can we learn from the Western thinking?

My most favored passage in the Bible is Psalm 119, which is the longest chapter therein. I believe it was written by Solomon, the wisest person ever lived. It contains 22 sections, and all verses in each section start with one Hebrew alphabet. In every verse, there is a special word exalting God's commands. These words include: law, testimonies, ways, precepts, statues, commandments, ordinances, and word, as shown in the following table:

English	Hebrew	Chinese	Forth
word	dabhar, imra	話	command
commandments	misvah	命令	primitive commands
law	torah	律法	teaching
testimonies	edah	法度	instructions
precepts	piqqudim	訓詞	lectures
statues	huqqim	律例	compound commands
ordinances	mishpatim	判語	command examples
ways	derek	道	exercises

The most striking word is word itself. In Forth, we consider commands as words, as those used in English to compose executable programs. Forth allows you to use words to create new words and therefore give you the power of creating new systems to solve all computational problems. Words thus embody intelligence and power, which can be manifested and amplified by computers.

In modern cultures, after the invention of printing press, words were slighted, even despised. They are just scribbles on paper, or noises filling the air. They have no weight, and they have little value. People use them to tell lies, and there is not respect to them. When you use words to write Forth programs, they are very different. They have meaning, they have value, and they actually cause things to happen. They remind you Genesis 1:3:

And God said: "Let there be light"; and there was light.

That's how powerful words should be.

In Psalm 119, you are encouraged to mediate on words and commands, study diligently on precepts, statues, and ordinances composed of words, and emulate existing testimonies to build words to solve your problem. It teaches you how to become a good programmer. If you read it in this light, it does not seem to be so monotonous or dry. It is especially soothing and encouraging, when you get struck in a program, and when the computer insists on doing what you say, not what you mean.

Another word in Psalm 119 which deeply impresses me is righteousness. Righteousness is an attribute of God, and cannot be achieved by us mortal beings, as much as we tried. As we struggle writing a program, our first and foremost goal is to get the problem solve correctly. However, correctness is necessary, but generally not satisfying. After the product is delivered, we will have some time to think about it, especially when bug reports start to pour in. As we keep on improving it, at some point, we will begin to sense rightness, which is satisfying. Rightness is attainable. Righteousness, probably not.

Then, what is rightness, really? It is simplicity, as Chuck Moore taught us:

"One principle that guided the evolution of Forth, and continues to guide its application, is bluntly: Keep It Simple. A simple solution has elegance. It is the result of exacting effort to understand the **real** problem and is recognized by its compelling sense of rightness. I stress this point because it contradicts the conventional view that power increases with complexity. Simplicity provides confidence, reliability, compactness, and speed." (From Forward in Leo Bradie's *Starting Forth*)

For 26 years, I have rewritten eForth many many times. In each re-write, I tried to make it simpler, and clearer. Now, in 86eForth v5.2, I think I have arrived rightness, and am very happy about it.

As Einstein said:

Everything Should Be Made as Simple as Possible, But Not Simpler.

Making 86eForth v5.2 any simpler probably would break it, or not useful as a programming tool.

Appendix 86eForth v5.2 Command Reference

Stack Comments:
Stack inputs and outputs are shown in the form: (input1 input2 ... - - output1 output2 ...)

Stack Abbreviations of Data Types
n	32 bit integer
d	64 bit integer
flag	Boolean flag, either 0 or -1
char	ASCII character or a byte
addr	32 bit address

Stack

?DUP	n -- n n | 0	Duplicate top of stack if it is not 0.
DUP	n1 -- n2	Duplicate top of stack.
DROP	n --	Discard top of stack.
SWAP	n1 n2 -- n2 n1	Exchange top two stack items.
OVER	n1 n2 -- n1 n2 n1	Make copy of second item on stack.
ROT	n1 n2 n3 -- n2 n3 n1	Rotate third item to top.
PICK	n -- n1	Zero based, duplicate nth item to top. (e.g. 0 PICK is DUP).
>R	n --	Move top item to return stack for temporary storage.
R>	-- n	Retrieve top item from return stack.
R@	-- n	Copy top of return stack onto stack.
2DUP	d -- d d	Duplicate double number on top of stack.
2DROP	d1 d2 --	Discard two double numbers on top of stack
DEPTH	-- n	Count number of items on stack.

Arithmetic

+	n1 n2 -- n3	Add n1 and n2.
-	n1 n2 -- n3	Subtract n2 from n1 (n1-n2=n3).
*	n1 n2 -- n3	Multiply. n3=n1*n2
/	n1 n2 -- n3	Division, signed (n3= n1/n2).
1+	n -- n+1	Increment n.
1-	n -- n-1	Decrement n.
2+	n -- n+2	Increment n by 2.
2-	n -- n-2	Decrement n by 2.
2*	n -- n*2	Logic left shift.
2/	n -- n/2	Logic right shift.
4+	n -- n+2	Increment n by 4.
4-	n -- n-2	Decrement n by 4.
4*	n -- n*2	Logic left shift 2 bits.
UM+	n1 n2 -- nd	Unsigned addition, double precision result.
UM*	n1 n2 -- nd	Unsigned multiply, double precision result.
M*	n n -- d	Signed multiply. Return double product.
UM/MOD	nd n1 -- mod quot	Unsigned division with double precision dividend.
M/MOD	d n -- mod quot	Signed floored divide of double by single. Return mod and quotient.
MOD	n1 n2 -- mod	Modulus, signed (remainder of n1/n2).
/MOD	n1 n2 -- mod quot	Division with both remainder and quotient.
*/MOD	n1 n2 n3 -- n4 n5	Multiply and then divide (n1*n2/n3)
*/	n1 n2 n3 -- n4	Like */MOD, but with quotient only.
ABS	n1 -- n2	If n1 is negative, n2 is its two's complement.
NEGATE	n1 -- n2	Two's complement.
DNEGATE	d1 -- d2	Negate double number. Two's complement.
D+	d1 d2 -- d3	Add double numbers.

Logic and Comparison

AND	n1 n2 -- n3	Logical bit-wise AND.
OR	n1 n2 -- n3	Logical bit-wise OR.
XOR	n1 n2 -- n3	Logical bit-wise exclusive OR.
NOT	n1 -- n2	Bit-wise one's complement.
0<	n -- flag	True if n is negative.
U<	n1 n2 -- flag	True if n1 less than n2. Unsigned compare.
<	n1 n2 -- flag	True if n1 less than n2.
=	n1 n2 -- flag	True if n1 equals n2.
MAX	n1 n2 -- n3	n3 is the larger of n1 and n2.
MIN	n1 n2 -- n3	n3 is the smaller of n1 and n2.
WITHIN	n1 n2 n3 -- flag	Return true if n1 is within range of n2 and n3. (n2 <= n1 < n3)

Memory

@	addr -- n	Replace addr by integer at addr.
C@	addr -- char	Fetch least-significant byte only.
!	n addr --	Store n at addr.
C!	char addr --	Store least-significant byte only.
2@	addr -- d	Fetch double integer d at addr.
2!	d addr --	Store double integer d at addr.
+!	n addr --	Add n to integer at addr.
COUNT	addr -- addr+1 char	Move string count from memory onto stack.
ALLOT	n --	Add n bytes to the RAM pointer DP.
HERE	-- addr	Address of next available RAM memory location.
PAD	-- addr	Address of a scratch area of at least 64 bytes.
TIB	-- addr	Address of terminal input buffer.
CMOVE	addr1 addr2 n --	Move n bytes starting at memory addr1 to addr2.
FILL	addr n char --	Fill n bytes of memory at addr with char.

ERASE	addr n --	Zero fill n bytes starting at addr
PACK$	addr1 u addr2 --	Build a string at addr2 from u characters at addr1

System Variables

SP0	-- addr	Origin of data stack
RP0	-- addr	Origin of return stack
BASE	-- addr	Radix for number conversion
TMP	-- addr	Temporary scratch pad
SPAN	-- addr	Actual number of characters received by EXPECT
>IN	-- addr	Character offset into the input stream buffer.
#TIB	-- addr	Current length of terminal input buffer (TIB.
'TIB	-- addr	Current address of terminal input buffer (TIB
'EVAL	-- addr	Interpreter or compiler to evaluate a command.
HLD	-- addr	Pointer to numeric string under construction.
CONTEXT	-- addr	Name field address of last command in dictionary
CP	-- addr	First free address in .data segment of memory
LAST	-- addr	Name field address of command under compilation

Terminal Input-Output

EMIT	char --	Display char.
KEY	-- char	Get an ASCII character from the keyboard.
?KEY	-- char -1 | 0	Return an ASCII character from the keyboard and a true flag. Return false flag if no character available.
.	n --	Display number n with a trailing blank.

U.	n --	Display an unsigned integer with a trailing blank.
.R	n1 n2 --	Display signed number n1 right justified in n2 character field.
U.R	n1 n2 --	Display unsigned number n1 right justified in n2 character field.
?	addr --	Display contents at memory addr.
<#	--	Start numeric output string conversion.
#	n1 -- n2	Convert next digit of number and add to output string
#S	n --	Convert all significant digits in n to output string.
HOLD	char --	Add char to output string.
SIGN	n --	If n is negative, add a minus sign to the output string.
#>	d -- addr n	Terminate numeric string, leaving addr and count for TYPE.
CR	--	Display a new line. Send carriage return and line feed.
SPACE	--	Display a space.
SPACES	n --	Display n spaces.
ACCEPT	addr n --	Accept n characters into buffer at addr.
TYPE	addr n --	Display a string of n characters starting at address addr.
BL	-- 32	Return ASCII Blank character.
DECIMAL	--	Set number base to decimal.
HEX	--	Set number base to hexadecimal.

Compiler and Interpreter

:<name>	--	Begin a colon definition of <name>.
;	--	Terminate execution of a colon definition.
CREATE <name>	--	Dictionary entry with no parameter field space reserved.
VARIABLE <name>	--	Defines a variable. At run-time, <name> leaves its address.
CONSTANT <name>	n --	Defines a constant. At run-time, n is left on the stack.

,	n --	Compile n to the dictionary in flash memory
IMMEDIATE	--	Cause last-defined command to execute even within a colon definition.
COMPILE <name>	--	<name> is compiled to dictionary.
[COMPILE] <name>	--	Immediate command. <name> is compiled to dictionary.
LITERAL	n --	Compile literal number n. At run-time, n is pushed on the stack.
[	--	Switch from compilation to interpretation.
]	--	Switch from interpretation to compilation.
WORD<text>	char -- addr	Get the char delimited string <text> from the input stream and leave as a counted string at addr.
(<comment>)	--	Ignore comment text.
**** <comment>	--	Ignore comment till end of line.
." <text>"	--	Compile <text> message. At run-time display text message.
.(<text>)	--	Display <text> from the input stream.
$" <text>"	-- addr	Compile <text> message. At run-time return its address.
ABORT" <text>"	flag --	Compile <test> message. At run-time display message and abort if flag is true. Otherwise, ignore message and continue.
COLD	--	Start eForth system.
QUIT	--	Return to interpret mode, clear data and return stacks.
QUERY	--	Accept input stream to terminal input buffer.
EXECUTE	addr --	Execute command definition at addr.
@EXECUTE	addr --	Execute command definition whose execution address is in addr.

Structures

IF	flag --	If flag is zero, branches forward to ELSE or THEN.
ELSE	--	Branch forward to THEN.
THEN	--	Terminate a IF-ELSE-THEN structure.
FOR	n --	Setup loop with n as index. Repeat loop n+1 times.
NEXT	--	Decrement loop index by 1 and branch back to FOR. Terminate FOR-NEXT loop when index is negative.
AFT	--	Branch forward to THEN in a loop to skip the first round
BEGIN	--	Start an indefinite loop.
AGAIN	--	Branch backward to BEGIN.
UNTIL	flag --	Branch backward to BEGIN if flag is false. If flag is true, terminate BEGIN-UNTIL loop.
WHILE	flag --	If flag is false, branch forward to terminate BEGIN-WHILE-REPEAT loop. If flag is true, continue execution till REPEAT.
REPEAT	--	Resolve WHILE clause. Branch backward to BEGIN.
AHEAD	--	Resolve WHILE clause. Branch backward to BEGIN.

Utility

' <name>	-- addr	Look up <name> in the dictionary. Return execution address.
DUMP	addr --	Dump 128 bytes of RAM memory starting from addr.
.S	--	Dump the parameter stack.
WORDS	--	Display all eForth commands
SEE	--	Decompile next word following SEE.
BYE	--	Terminate eForth and return to Windows.

Inner Interpreters

$NEXT	--	A macro assembling LODSD JMP [EAX] at end of code word
DOLST	--	Address interpreter to start executing following token list
EXIT	--	Terminate execution of a token list
DOVAR	-- addr	Variable interpreter to return parameter field address
DOCON	-- n	Constant interpreter to return value in parameter field
DOLIT	-- n	Integer literal interpreter to return following literal value
BRANCH	--	Unconditionally branch to following literal address
?BRANCH	flag --	Branch to following literal address if flag is false
DONXT	--	Decrement count on return stack. Branch to following literal address if count is not negative; else pop return stack and exit loop.
DO$	-- addr	Return address of a compiled string literal
$"|	-- addr	String literal interpreter returning address of following string
."|	--	String literal interpreter displaying following string
ABORT"|	flag --	If flag is true, display following string and ABORT.

Supporting Words

SP@	-- addr	Push the current data stack pointer on stack.
SP!	addr --	Set the data stack pointer to addr.
RP@	-- addr	Push the current RP on the data stack.
RP!	addr --	Set the return stack pointer to addr.

DIGIT	u -- char	Convert digit u to a character.
EXTRACT	n1 base – n2 char	Extract the least significant digit from n1. Leave quotient n2 and digit char.
>CHAR	char -- char	Filter non-printing character to an underscore.
STR	n – addr count	Convert a signed integer to a numeric string.
DIGIT?	char base– n flag	Convert a character to its numeric value. A flag indicates success.
NUF?	-- flag	Return false if no input, else pause and if CR return true.
(PARSE)	addr n char – addr n delta	Scan string delimited by c. Return found string and its offset delta.
PARSE	char – addr n	Scan input stream and return counted string delimited by char.
TOKEN	-- addr	Parse a word from input stream and copy it to name dictionary.
NUMBER?	addr -- n -1 | addr 0	Convert a number string to integer. Push a flag on data stack.
NAME>	nfa -- cfa	Return a code field address given a name field address.
>NAME	cfa -- nfa	Convert code field address to a name field address.
NAME?	addr -- cfa nfa | addr flag	Search dictionary for a string at addr. Return cfa and nfa if found. Else push a false flag above addr
SAME?	a1 a2 n – a1 a2 flag	Compare u-2 bytes in two strings. Return 0 if identical.
FIND	a va -- cfa nfa | a flag	Search a dictionary for a string. Return cfa and nfa if succeeded. Else, return a and false flag.
^H	bot eot cur -- bot eot cur	Backup the cursor by one character.
TAP	bot eot cur char -- bot eot cur	Accept and echo the key stroke and bump the cursor.
kTAP	bot eot cur char -- bot eot cur	Process a key stroke, CR or backspace.
?STACK	--	Abort if the data stack underflows.

.OK	--	Display the data stack only while interpreting.
EVAL	--	Interpret the input stream.
PRESET	--	Reset data stack pointer.
$INTERPRET	addr --	Interpret a word. If failed, try to convert it to an integer. Failing that, ABORT
$COMPILE	addr --	Compile a word to dictionary as a token or literal. Failing both, ABORT
?UNIQUE	addr -- addr	Display a warning message if the word at addr already exists.
$,"	--	Compile a literal string up to next " .
$,n	addr --	Build a new dictionary name using the string at addr
OVERT	--	Link a new word into the current dictionary.
.ID	nfa --	Display the name at name field address.

####

Dr. Chen-Hanson Ting

Introduction:
Retired chemist-turned-engineer

How long have you been interested in Forth:
32 years

Bio:

PhD in chemistry, University of Chicago, 1965.
Professor of chemistry in Taiwan until 1975.

Firmware engineer in Silicon Valley until retirement in 2000. Still actively composing Forth Haikus.

Custodian of the eForth systems since 1990,
still maintaining eForth systems for Arduino, MSP430, and various ARM microcontrollers.

Author of eP8, eP16, eP24, and eP32 microcontrollers in VHDL, which were implemented on several FPGA chips.

Offete Enterprises, started in 1975, and is now formally closed. However, Dr. Ting can still be contacted
through email chenhting@yahoo.com.tw

(source www.forth.org/whoswho.html#chting)

Exeter UK - ExMark   Juergen Pintaske - February 2017